Building Web Apps for Google TV

Building Web Apps for Google TV

Andrés Ferraté, Amanda Surya, Daniels Lee, Maile Ohye,
Paul Carff, Shawn Shen, and Steven Hines

O'REILLY®

Beijing · Cambridge · Farnham · Köln · Sebastopol · Tokyo

Building Web Apps for Google TV

by Andrés Ferraté, Amanda Surya, Daniels Lee, Maile Ohye, Paul Carff, Shawn Shen, and Steven Hines

Published by O'Reilly Media, Inc., 1005 Gravenstein Highway North, Sebastopol, CA 95472.

O'Reilly books may be purchased for educational, business, or sales promotional use. Online editions are also available for most titles (*http://my.safaribooksonline.com*). For more information, contact our corporate/institutional sales department: (800) 998-9938 or *corporate@oreilly.com*.

Editors: Mike Hendrickson and Mary Treseler	**Cover Designer:** Karen Montgomery
Production Editor: Jasmine Perez	**Interior Designer:** David Futato
Proofreader: Jasmine Perez	**Illustrator:** Robert Romano

Printing History:

June 2011:	First Edition.

Nutshell Handbook, the Nutshell Handbook logo, and the O'Reilly logo are registered trademarks of O'Reilly Media, Inc. *Building Web Apps for Google TV*, the image of the musk deer, and related trade dress are trademarks of O'Reilly Media, Inc.

Many of the designations used by manufacturers and sellers to distinguish their products are claimed as trademarks. Where those designations appear in this book, and O'Reilly Media, Inc. was aware of a trademark claim, the designations have been printed in caps or initial caps.

While every precaution has been taken in the preparation of this book, the publisher and authors assume no responsibility for errors or omissions, or for damages resulting from the use of the information contained herein.

ISBN: 978-1-449-30457-7

[LSI]

1308854690

Table of Contents

Foreword

When designing Google TV, we wanted to address some of the pain points we had experienced as television viewers. We all had our own favorite TV shows; we enjoyed friends coming over to watch the Super Bowl; we loved watching movies on a large screen in the comfort of our homes. Yet, we knew that many of the TV shows and movies produced never find their way through traditional distribution channels to our living rooms. We wanted to bring the infinite shelf space provided by the Internet to television, carrying with it all of the TV shows and movies ever produced. We also wanted to make it dead simple to find something great to watch, whether from a TV channel or Internet source. Last but not least, we wanted the big screen in our living rooms to be more than a TV. We wanted it to be a space where we could share photos, music, and more with our family and friends, sitting next to each other on a couch.

These were ambitious goals that we felt we could not reach on our own. We set ourselves on a course to build a platform to empower developers like you to innovate and propel television into the second decade of the 21st century. This is how Google TV was born. Do you remember the ancient days when all you could do with a phone was place and answer calls and send short messages? These times seem long gone even though the revolution of smart phones started less than three years ago. We are inviting you to become the foot soldiers, admirals, and visionaries of the smart TV revolution. Furthermore, there are over four billion and growing television viewers. For many of them, television is their only window into the world. We are counting on you to give all of them more programs to watch on TV, better ways to find what to watch on TV, and more things to do with their TVs.

Perhaps one day Bruce Springsteen will have to update his famous line: "Billions of web pages and nothing to watch." Somehow we believe you will make sure that never happens.

—Vincent Dureau
Head of TV Technology, on behalf of the Google TV team

Preface

This book provides an in-depth look at how to build web-based applications (web apps) for Google TV, a new platform that integrates the open web with traditional TV. This powerful and versatile new platform includes Google Chrome, a modern web browser that enables developers to deliver rich and sophisticated web apps to Google TV users.

This book has three primary goals. First, this book aims to familiarize web developers with the Google TV platform. Second, this book aims to share knowledge about the various ways in which developers can create web apps for Google TV. Lastly, this book aims to inform web developers about tools and techniques that are useful for the implementation of web apps geared for the Google TV platform.

Once you read this book, you'll understand the Google TV platform and you'll have the knowledge and skills needed to build web apps for Google TV.

About This Book

This book is a resource for web developers. The book presents an early look at a new platform that aims to provide users with a new and exciting way to access the web from their living rooms. As the Google TV platform evolves, the technical knowledge you'll gain from this book will allow you to offer a variety of user experiences on applications that are delivered through the Google TV version of the Google Chrome browser.

This Book's Target Audience

This book primarily is aimed at a technical audience, especially web developers who have previous experience working with web apps that utilize Ajax, HTML5, and/or Adobe Flash. Although previous experience developing web apps is valuable, it is not necessary, and we've included pointers throughout to book to resources that will get you up to speed quickly.

This Book's Scope

We've divided this book into three sections. Chapters 1 and 2 cover the conceptual knowledge you need to understand the Google TV platform and the basics of web development for the platform. Chapters 3, 4, and 5 dive into technical discussion about design, development, and implementaion of web apps. Chapters 6 and 7 cover relevant information about how to tune and distribute your content, as well as how to make it discoverable.

Google TV presents a new opportunity for web developers to work on an emerging corner of the open web: the *TV* web. Google TV is one of the first technologies to bring a full web browser to TV, allowing for some really great user experiences. However, as developers have discovered with the mobile web, there are nuances to making the web accessible on devices other than desktop and laptop computers. In similar fashion, there are nuances for building web apps for the TV web.

User experiences that you have come to assume for other devices do not necessarily translate to the TV web and likewise the TV web also encompasses user experiences that are not associated with mobile or desktop web apps. As you familiarize yourself with Google TV and the context in which users access web apps, you'll begin to realize that content and features need to be catered to what many folks refer to as the *10-foot experience*.

Prerequisites

General familiarity with web development is valuable, although not absolutely necessary. If you have worked with HTML and Javascript, Flash, and Google Chrome, you'll find the knowledge and information in this book easier to understand and assimilate.

Conventions Used in This Book

The following typographical conventions are used in this book:

Italic
> Indicates new terms, URLs, email addresses, filenames, and file extensions.

`Constant width`
> Used for program listings, as well as within paragraphs to refer to program elements such as variable or function names, databases, data types, environment variables, statements, and keywords.

`Constant width bold`
> Shows commands or other text that should be typed literally by the user.

`Constant width italic`
> Shows text that should be replaced with user-supplied values or by values determined by context.

This icon signifies a tip, suggestion, or general note.

 This icon indicates a warning or caution.

Using Code Examples

This book is here to help you get your job done. In general, you may use the code in this book in your programs and documentation. You do not need to contact us for permission unless you're reproducing a significant portion of the code. For example, writing a program that uses several chunks of code from this book does not require permission. Selling or distributing a CD-ROM of examples from O'Reilly books does require permission. Answering a question by citing this book and quoting example code does not require permission. Incorporating a significant amount of example code from this book into your product's documentation does require permission.

We appreciate, but do not require, attribution. An attribution usually includes the title, author, publisher, and ISBN. For example: "*Building Web Apps for Google TV* by Andrés Ferraté, Amanda Surya, Daniels Lee, Maile Ohye, Paul Carff, Shawn Shen, and Steven Hines. Copyright 2011 Andrés Ferraté, Amanda Surya, Daniels Lee, Maile Ohye, Paul Carff, Shawn Shen, and Steven Hines, 978-1-449-30457-7."

If you feel your use of code examples falls outside fair use or the permission given above, feel free to contact us at *permissions@oreilly.com*.

Safari® Books Online

 Safari Books Online is an on-demand digital library that lets you easily search over 7,500 technology and creative reference books and videos to find the answers you need quickly.

With a subscription, you can read any page and watch any video from our library online. Read books on your cell phone and mobile devices. Access new titles before they are available for print, and get exclusive access to manuscripts in development and post feedback for the authors. Copy and paste code samples, organize your favorites, download chapters, bookmark key sections, create notes, print out pages, and benefit from tons of other time-saving features.

O'Reilly Media has uploaded this book to the Safari Books Online service. To have full digital access to this book and others on similar topics from O'Reilly and other publishers, sign up for free at *http://my.safaribooksonline.com*.

How to Contact Us

Please address comments and questions concerning this book to the publisher:

O'Reilly Media, Inc.
1005 Gravenstein Highway North
Sebastopol, CA 95472
800-998-9938 (in the United States or Canada)
707-829-0515 (international or local)
707-829-0104 (fax)

We have a web page for this book, where we list errata, examples, and any additional information. You can access this page at:

http://www.oreilly.com/catalog/0636920019886

To comment or ask technical questions about this book, send email to:

bookquestions@oreilly.com

For more information about our books, courses, conferences, and news, see our website at *http://www.oreilly.com.*

Find us on Facebook: *http://facebook.com/oreilly*

Follow us on Twitter: *http://twitter.com/oreillymedia*

Watch us on YouTube: *http://www.youtube.com/oreillymedia*

Acknowledgments

We would like to sincerely thank the entire Google TV team for its hard and tireless work on the creation of a new platform that already has yielded a new wave of apps geared for the 10-foot experience. We'd also like to thank the entire O'Reilly Media team for their collaboration and assistance with the production of this book. Lastly, we'd like to thank the countless developers out there that continue to innovate, produce, and deliver solutions that make the open web valuable and meaningful.

CHAPTER 1

Introducing Google TV

Even before Google TV was launched, the same questions seemed to be on everyone's mind: What exactly is Google TV? Is it a new TV channel? Is it a new LCD TV made by Google? Is it a subscription service? What can you do with it? The answer is actually simple: Google TV is a new platform that seamlessly combines the web with television. As you'll find in this and subsequent chapters, Google TV is an open and flexible platform that gives you, the developer, various avenues for bringing rich applications to the TV via the web.

Google TV runs on the Android platform, the same platform that powers millions of mobile devices. And Google TV ships with Google Chrome, Google's own open-source browser which supports both HTML5 and Adobe Flash*. This means that there are essentially two paths to build applications for Google TV: you can build web applications (apps) for Chrome or you can develop Android applications. This book is aimed at developers who are interested in creating web apps for Google TV, although many of the design and user experience considerations also are relevant for Android apps.

> The Google Chrome browser is a key differentiator between Google TV and other "smart TVs," as Google TV is the only platform that includes a full web browser. We feel that Google Chrome gives developers a great advantage, as they can create rich and sophisticated applications using existing technologies and approaches already compatible with Google Chrome and other "modern" web browsers, rather than developing widgets or apps that run on feature-limited browsers.

---

* The Google TV platform supports videos rendered in Adobe Flash format. Visit Adobe's developer website at *http://www.adobe.com/devnet/devices/* for further information on developing content using Adobe Flash technology.

So is it better to develop web apps or Android apps? This seems to be a question on every developer's mind as he or she decides to embark on creating an app for Google TV. There is no single answer, but you should consider the following factors (also keep in mind that the Google TV SDK add-on for Android is not yet available):

Type of application you want to build and type of content you want to feature	If your content/app only streams videos or other multimedia content, then going the web/Google Chrome route is often the easiest way to go. On the other hand, if you want to build an app that integrates deeply with the existing system, then building an Android app is the way to go.
	An Android app can take advantage of more native feature such as integration with Google TV's Quick Search Box, where applications can contribute to the global search result displayed to end users.
Developer's skill set	Building an Android application requires a pretty different skill set from building a web application. Android app development requires knowledge of the Java programming language, while web development typically requires knowledge of JavaScript, HTML, CSS, and/or Flash.
	Most apps will require ongoing enhancements and maintenance post-launch, so as a developer, you need to decide which programming language you are most comfortable using.
Timeline for release	Building a web app for Google Chrome can typically be accomplished faster than building an Android app, especially if you already have a website. Some developers have turned around a TV "optimized" site in a matter of two to three weeks. If your site conforms to web standards that Google Chrome supports, it will likely perform well.
	Android app development, on the other hand, requires more time to perfect. Android apps may also require some upgrade paths as the platform itself is upgraded with subequent versions of Android.
Monetization strategy	Monetization is a topic that often gets a developer's attention. The prominent monetization strategy for web apps on Google TV at this point is to show ads on the optimized site. "Pre-rolls" can be shown in videos or banner and Adsense type ads can be displayed on a site.
	You could also use a freemium model where you present free content as well as paid content behind a paywall. If the paywall conforms to web standards that Google Chrome supports, normal web-based transactions (e.g., using Google Checkout, PayPal, etc.) should work.
	For Android apps, Google TV will integrate Android Market, where developers can offer up their apps for TV for a price. Developers also will eventually have the option to display ads on Android apps installed on Google TV.

Build Both a Web App and an Android App?

The decision to build a web app or Android app doesn't necessarily have to come down to one or the other. You may find in some instances that you need to offer both a web app and an Android app in order to ensure that users have a good experience, regardless of whether they're accessing your content via the Google Chrome browser or an app installed from Android Market. A fitting metaphor here is the mobile web and how popular destinations on the web provide access to their content with both web apps optimized for mobile browsers and apps downloaded from markets.

Under the Hood: So What's in There?

Let's see what exactly powers the Google TV platform. At the time of this writing, the latest version of Google TV commercially available is v1.3, released in March 2011 and, as we already mentioned, there are essentially three key elements of the platform: the Android operating system, Google Chrome, and Flash.

Android

Android is a powerful and versatile platform, and for Google TV, it has been adapted to take full advantage of the TV form factor and the various types of content typically accessed on TV. In adapting Android for Google TV, certain features that are not as relevant to TV are not exposed, including:

- Touch Screen
- Accelerometer
- Gyroscope
- Bluetooth
- GPS

Google TV will continue to evolve and it is expected that subsequent versions of the platform will integrate features and functionality that become available on future versions of the Android. You can learn more about Android at

http://developer.android.com.

Google Chrome 5.0

The browser on Google TV is simply the Linux version of Google Chrome. While the user interface is modified slightly for the TV form factor, most of the rendering and web platform capabilities are consistent with desktop versions of Google Chrome, and users receive the latest updates automatically.

Flash 10.1 Beta

A beta version of Flash Player 10.1 for Google TV is built directly into the Google Chrome browser. To ensure that users always have the latest version of Flash Player running on their home devices, the Flash Player will be updated by Google over the air as new versions of the Google TV platform are released.

You can read more details of Flash 10.1 capabilities on Adobe's website at:

http://goo.gl/YWm1z

User Interface

Note that the Google TV user interface consists of two main components, each offering access to content. The quick search bar (QSB) is universally accessible at any point and it is seamlessly integrated with TV content, allowing users to easily search for content (and apps) while they're watching TV (Figure 1-1). The home dashboard (Figure 1-2) gives users access to a variety of content, including apps (such as Google Chrome), bookmarks, and syndicated media (such as podcasts and videocasts).

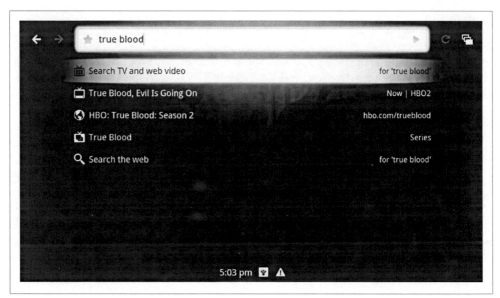

Figure 1-1. The QSB shows a blend of search results from traditional TV and the web

Figure 1-2. Users are able to access and bookmark everything from websites to apps on Google TV; note the various "live folders" on the left

A New Target Device

You may or may not remember designing websites for those old CRT monitors (you know, the ones with VGA connections that had a maximum resolution of 640 × 480 pixels). Back then, there were only a few target devices for which you designed and developed websites. Fast-forward to the present day: the web is accessible from an ever increasing number of devices. Desktops, laptops, smart phones, tablets, and even MP3 players have built in browsers.

It's no longer a matter of ensuring that your website or web app works well with different browsers; you also have to make sure that it works well on relatively small displays, such as those found on smart phones, and large displays, such as those sexy new LCD monitors that you just got at work. And now TVs are a target device. We know: it's exciting, yet mildly daunting at the same time.

The TV is the latest target device to come on the web scene. It's also the best and most easily accessible display in the house.

It's More Than Just a Big Monitor

One of the first assumptions that some developers make about building web apps for TV is that the target device is just another monitor, albeit a bigger one. While that comparison may be true when it comes to display technology and general form factor, the similarities end when it comes to user interaction and the presentation of content.

The term "10-foot experience" is typically used to allude to the idea that users will be at least 10 feet away when interacting with a TV. When you start to think about how this contrasts with the average use of a monitor display (whether on a laptop or a desktop), it becomes obvious that your web app needs to accomodate the TV, both its physical properties as well as its expected use. Showing curated content from Wikipedia (especially images or snippets of articles) or showing a nice chart for some statistic is viable for a web app geared for TV; however, it's unlikely that you'll find too many people interested in reading full-length Wikipedia articles or crunching numbers on a complex spreadsheet on TV.

Input Devices (or How to Control That Google TV)

In addition to its integration with TVs, Google TV relies on input devices to control the user interface, much the same way that a touchpad is used to control a cursor on a laptop or touch gestures are used to control a smart phone.

These input devices range in design and form factor (in some instances they are virtual), but they all share common controls. You can count on users being able to access the following types of controls on a device with Google TV:

- Full keyboard
- Mouse or equivalent, including trackpads
- Media transport controls, including play, pause, stop, next, previous, fast-forward, and rewind
- Directional pad, otherwise known as a D-Pad or 5-way navigation that includes left, right, top, bottom, and enter buttons

Physical devices currently available include Logitech's wireless keyboard (Figure 1-3) and Sony's handheld wireless remote (Figure 1-4).

 You can familiarize yourself with the Google TV user interface by viewing the "What Is Google TV?" video on YouTube (*http://goo.gl/SSdQN*).

Figure 1-3. The wireless keyboard that ships with the Logitech Revue

Figure 1-4. Sony's handheld remote control for its TVs and Blu-ray player that come with Google TV

Remember When...

The mobile device revolution is still playing out, but we don't have to look too far back to see how mobile devices have evolved, and, in particular, how Android has evolved. Remember when the T-Mobile G1 first hit the market in October 2008? It was the first smart phone powered by Android to go on sale (Figure 1-5).

Figure 1-5. The T-Mobile G1, manufactured by HTC, led the way for the more than 60 Android compatible mobile devices available today. Image courtesy HTC, Inc.

The phone itself was not necessarily revolutionary, but it did serve to preview a revolutionary mobile platform. And the technology industry took note, as is evident from the reviews that appeared after the G1 was released:

- *PC Mag* called it "a basic introduction to what could be a blockbuster mobile platform. While it lacks key features right now, it's a decent smartphone that will surely grow with time."[†]
- *CNET* wrote "the real beauty of the T-Mobile G1 is the Google Android platform, as it has the potential to make smartphones more personal and powerful. That

[†] *T-Mobile G1 (Google Android Phone)*. PC Mag, 2008. *http://goo.gl/GQzIi*

said, it's not quite there yet, so for now, the G1 is best suited for early adopters and gadget hounds, rather than consumers and business users."‡

- *Engadget* summed up its review with "The story here is Android and what it promises … though doesn't necessarily deliver on at first. Like any paradigm shift, it's going to take time. There is tremendous potential for this OS on mobile devices—it truly realizes the open ideals laid out by Google when they announced this project."§

Less than two years later, in June 2010, there were over 60 compatible Android mobile devices (from 21 original equipment manufacturers [OEMs] in 48 countries with 59 carriers) that had embraced the Android platform. Moreover, every day approximately 300,000 Android-powered devices are activated, and the Android market itself has over 100,000 apps. That's impressive and beyond what many in the Android team expected.

Google TV as a platform is still in its early days. The first version was released in October 2010 and in some ways it is analogous to the G1. Similarly, the potential is there for the Google TV platform to grow and blossom into more devices from more OEMs in more countries, thereby reaching millions of consumers.

An Emerging Opportunity for Developers

From mobile devices that use native apps and mobile browsers to access web apps to Flash applications on a desktop to static websites, developers continue to expand the reach of their creativity and innovation (not to mention entrepreneurship!). The reach of the web continues to expand as more web-capable devices emerge and users continue to gain access to the Internet. Google TV builds on this momentum and brings forth an opportunity for developers to deliver applications that bring further access to the web on the largest screen in the household: the TV.

Just the Facts

You've probably heard or read about this statistic somewhere, but people seem to watch a lot of TV, especially North Americans. A recent Nielsen study found that people on average watched nearly five hours of TV per day in the U.S. during the first half of 2010 (this includes adults and children).‖ As for the Internet, adults in the U.S. spent an average of 13 hours per week online in 2010.# In fact, according to Forrester Research, in 2010, adults in the U.S. for the first time spent as much time online as they did

---

‡ *T-Mobile G1 (black)*. CNET, 2008. *http://goo.gl/7Diuz*

§ *T-Mobile G1 review, part 2: software and wrap-up*. Engadget, 2008. *http://goo.gl/ly7mN*

‖ The Nielsen Company. *State of the Media, TV Usage Trends: Q2 2010*. 2010. *http://goo.gl/TnhZ6*

Understanding The Changing Needs Of The US Online Consumer, 2010. Jacqueline Anderson et al. Forrester Research, Inc. December 13, 2010.

watching TV.# Take into account that there are approximately 115 million households in the U.S. with at least one TV (Figure 1-6)*, many of whom already have or soon will have broadband access (Figure 1-7). The potential reach for web apps geared for TV is quite large, and we've only touched on statistics for the U.S.† On a worldwide basis, about three-quarters of every household has a TV and approximately one billion people have access to the Internet.‡

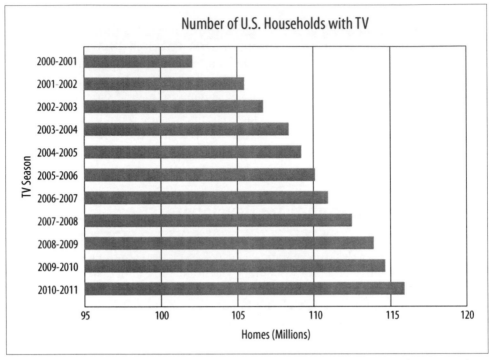

Figure 1-6. The number of households with a TV in the U.S. continues to grow, with a projected one million additional households in 2010–2011. Source: The Nielsen Company. Number of U.S. TV Households Climbs by One Million for 2010-11 TV Season. August 27, 2010. http://goo.gl/ITaTK

---

* The Nielsen Company. *2010 Media Industry Fact Sheet*. 2010. *http://goo.gl/wPTj*

† Keep in mind that Google TV is currently only available in the U.S.

‡ *THE WORLD IN 2009: ICT Facts and Figures*. International Telecommunication Union, 2009.

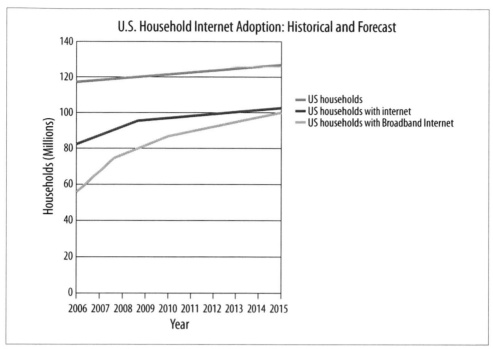

Figure 1-7. Households across the U.S. are increasingly gaining access to broadband Internet. Almost 80% of households in the U.S. have an Internet connection, and in 2010, approximately 90% of those households had a broadband Internet connection. Source: Understanding The Changing Needs Of The US Online Consumer, 2010. Jacqueline Anderson et al. Forrester Research, Inc. December 13, 2010.

Consider for a moment that we're at the early stages of a convergence between TV and the web. The web encompasses a broad set of content, much of which is relevant for consumption on TV. Now imagine for a moment that a platform like Google TV gives users access to both traditional TV programming and content on the web in a seamless way.

Users aren't likely to care so much about the source of the content, but rather the content itself. And it's this seamless integration that gives developers a new avenue for web apps that provide access to content and features alongside traditional TV.

We've established that there's a large audience of people that have both a TV and broadband Internet access. So what kinds of content should your web app deliver?

Video is an obvious fit for TV, and online video is certainly a popular media type on the web. Consider that in October 2010 over 84% of the U.S. Internet audience (175 million people or so) viewed online video (with an average video length of five minutes).[§] If you've got video content or you can integrate video content, this is certainly one media type not to exclude from your web app.

You may also want to consider audio content. TVs typically tend to be hooked up to home entertainment systems and thus audio content delivered to a TV can be enjoyed on a system that plays audio well. Images, especially photos, also lend themselves well to TV. The web is full of user-contributed images on sites like Flickr and Picasa, as well as professional and computer-generated images, all of which tend to display well on TV.

Games also present another opportunity for web apps on Google TV. Games are a popular online activity in the U.S., second only to social networks.|| There already is a booming industry for console games for TV, and in general these are not the type of games that you would replicate with a web app (nor would it be fair to compare Google TV to a game console). However, casual and social games do lend themselves well to web apps and Google TV.

Other content may also be appropriate, relevant, and compelling to a TV audience. Since the relatively recent release of Google TV, there have already been several web apps produced that deliver some interesting content on TV, including children's books, newspapers, and sports statistics. The key to determining what content will work well on Google TV is to place yourself in your living room and to think about what parts of the web you'd like to see most on your TV.

 Be sure to research specific audience demographics to determine whether the app you're building is a good fit for a traditional TV audience.

Working with the Open Web

At the Google I/O conference in May 2010, Google announced that user adoption for its Chrome browser had been steadily growing over the last year, reaching over 70 million active users. Fast-forward to December 2010, when Google's Chrome team announced that the browser now has over 120 million active users (pretty good numbers for a browser that was released to the public two years prior). It seems that an increasing number of users are finding Google Chrome to be useful, and the inclusion of this "modern" browser on the Google TV platform is good news for developers as well.

Remember that the Chrome browser on Google TV includes support for rich web apps through both HTML5 and Flash. This means that just about any website on the web can be displayed on Google TV, making the web accessible the way that it was originally intended to be: as an open network. There are no restrictions on what can be accessed via the Chrome browser on Google TV, and this bodes well for you, the developer, as

§ *comScore Releases October 2010 U.S. Online Video Rankings.* comScore, 2010. *http://goo.gl/ASqYR*

|| The Nielsen Company. *What Americans Do Online: Social Media And Games Dominate Activity.* August 2, 2010. *http://goo.gl/6ynoZ*

it means that there is no approval process or new set of technologies that stand in your way of getting something valuable and compelling out into the open web.

A Web App Is Worth a Thousand...

Thus far, we've touched on some conceptual discussion about the opportunity that Google TV presents for developers. A potentially large audience, the open web, a modern browser: these are all parts of the opportunity to bring web apps to the living room.

There is also an opportunity to innovate with regard to these web apps, as is evident by the increasing number of web apps that have been created or customized for Google TV. This is a new category of web apps that are catered for use on a TV. Here's a brief overview to give you a feel for what types of web apps developers have produced for Google TV.

YouTube Leanback

The YouTube web app for Google TV is aptly named *YouTube Leanback*. The app is Flash-based and it is one of the first web apps that was specifically developed for Google TV. As you can see, the contrast between the standard YouTube UI (Figure 1-8) and YouTube Leanback (Figure 1-9) is quite significant.

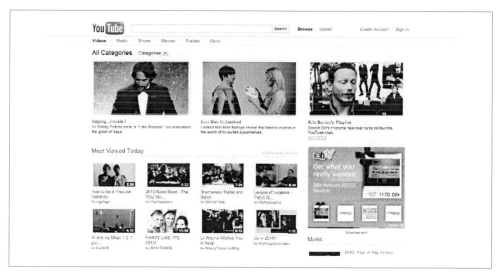

Figure 1-8. The standard YouTube UI

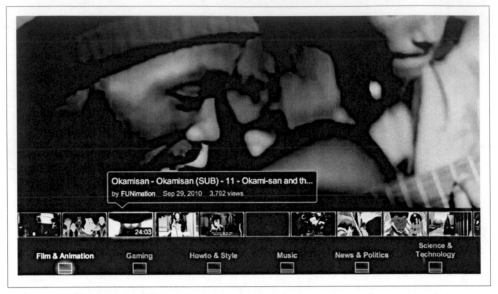

Figure 1-9. YouTube's Leanback UI

Since its release, the YouTube Leanback UI has served as a model for other web apps that are focused on video. Emphasis is on graphical elements and the videos automatically launch in full-screen. You can check out this web app on your Google TV or web browser at *http://www.youtube.com/leanback*.

Meegenius

Meegenius is an online children's book service that includes several enhancements, including word highlighting and audio playback. Traditional stories such as *The Three Little Pigs* and *The Boy Who Cried Wolf* are displayed as text, while the words of the book are highlighted as the stories are read aloud by a human voice. Meegenius has developed a web app for Google TV that is based on an existing suite of apps, and the experience they deliver highlights the accessibility and relevance of niche content on TV.

Figure 1-10 shows the Meegenius "bookshelf," an index of stories that can be selected and viewed on Google TV. When a user selects a story (Figure 1-11), the UI moves into a virtual book mode wherein stories are read out loud while words are highlighted. The use case here is compelling, and it combines virtual learning with TV.

Figure 1-10. The Meegenius bookshelf places emphasis on titles and thumbnails, and it is D-Pad navigable

Figure 1-11. Taking a look at The Boy Who Cried Wolf on the Meegenius web app

Flixster

Flixster is a social recommendation engine for movies that also provides movie reviews from Rotten Tomatoes. This web app uses HTML5 for the UI (Figure 1-12) and Flash to stream movie trailers in full screen.

Figure 1-12. Flixster's elegant UI makes it easy to drill down and access content for a variety of movies

When taking a look at this web app on Google TV, the lines between a native app and web app blur quite a bit, and unless you were to take a look at the browser's address bar, you would have a hard time telling that this is a web app.

The Next Killer App

You've likely heard of the smart phone and tablet apps that rose to popularity with the introduction of the Android market as well as Apple's App Store—apps like Pandora, Angry Birds, and Talking Tom Cat. These apps have flourished because users have adopted new devices and these users have gravitated to apps that provide unique and compelling experiences.

Likewise, as the web finds its way to an increasing number of TVs, users will be in search of the next set of killer apps for the large TV screen. What will those be? What can they do? How much can you charge for it? We don't know the answers yet, but as with any new platform, developers like yourself will help to shape the future of apps on television.

CHAPTER 2

Getting Started

In the previous chapter, we introduced you to Google TV and we discussed the opportunity that this new platform presents for developers. We're still in the early days of the platform, but even now it's evident that Google TV has the potential to become a revolutionary platform that provides developers with another avenue to distribute content. The web and TV are a natural fit, and their integration via Google TV has opened up a new avenue for developers to build and deliver a compelling experience for users.

Before we dive into a technical discussion in the next chapter, we'd like to ensure that you have some context and background that will help you as you get started. This is an opportunity to pass on some wisdom that will make your life easier as you build an app for Google TV.

What Makes a Compelling App?

As we discussed in the previous chapter, we're talking about a lot more than just thinking of a TV as a big monitor. Imagine how you, your family and friends, and billions of other people around the world interact daily with a TV. The possibilities are enormous and yet building a compelling app for TV, not just Google TV, may not be as easy as it sounds.

Let's take a look at some key characteristics that we think contribute to the popularity and value of web apps for Google TV.

Compelling Content

The web is full of all kinds of content, and the amount of content being generated and added to the web is staggering. The number of web pages worldwide grew by 21.4 million in 2010 to reach 255 million web pages.[*] How much of this is valuable and

---

[*] *Internet 2010 in Numbers.* January 12, 2011. Royal Pingdom. *http://goo.gl/8JXku*

compelling content? Obviously that is a subjective question, but the idea behind delivering compelling content on Google TV depends on three factors: audience, quality, and relevance. Your goal is to demand the user's attention.

Identifying your audience is just as important as the actual content that you plan on delivering. Take some time to think about who will be consuming your content. Is it college students, baby boomers, children, professionals, techies, new moms, or all of the above? While this may seem straightforward, you'll need to determine early on whether your content is universally compelling or whether it is compelling to a niche audience. There is no right answer or approach to this, but the key is to identify what your audience will want to access. Is it cute videos of kittens playing with yarn, how-to-cook videos, beautiful photographs of landscapes, news headlines, or a casual game?

If you have a popular website, say something like a blog, consider whether the audience for your blog will be the same one that accesses the web app you build for Google TV. Figure 2-1 shows a web app for CHOW, a culinary TV channel that offers users short-length tips and how-to videos for the kitchen.

Figure 2-1. CHOW offers a variety of useful content, including a set of videos that tell users what not to do in the kitchen

Quality is a subjective factor, but ensuring that your content displays and works well on large screens is crucial. Remember, your target device is the best and largest screen in the house, so your content should meet user expectations. This logic applies to the content as well as to assets (graphics) and other elements that are used in your UI. You can have great video content for example, but your app will be a letdown if it has small buttons or pixelated images as part of the UI. Vimeo's "couchmode" experience demonstrates a good combination of content and UI elements, and it launches high definition videos in full screen by default (Figure 2-2).

Figure 2-2. Vimeo's 10-foot experience focuses on delivering high definition videos

What about relevance? How can relevance be determined? It will become clear quickly if your content is not relevant to the audience you've identified or if the content is not relevant to TV in general. For example, you may have aggregated a lot of user-generated content (UGC) on a website about civil war history. Depending on the nature of the content, it may or may not be relevant to an audience. C-SPAN.org, a popular website with content focused on U.S. government and public affairs activity, has produced a web app for Google TV that features its most relevant content: its videos (Figure 2-3).

Figure 2-3. There is not doubt that C-SPAN.org's web app is relevant for a niche audience interested in government and public affairs

Say that you have a dedicated group of war history buffs that has a significant online presence. Great, that is a readily identifiable target demographic. But if most of your content is dense text and poorly drawn maps of battlefields, then the content is not relevant to the target device. Lots of text is not ideal for reading on TV and neither are graphics that don't display well.

A Low Learning Curve

One of the commonalities that we've seen for web apps that get a good reception from users is the streamlining of features and functionality. It's great if your app has lots of features and functionality, but these should not be exposed all at once. Giving users the ability to discover more complex features and functionality is a fundamental aspect of good UX design in the present day.

Remember that TV has traditionally been a passive device (until now) and users are accustomed to using a D-Pad to interact in simple ways with their TVs. Asking them to use keyboard shortcuts or including twenty menu items on the main UI makes the learning curve steeper. Your goal is to let users explore your app so that they can gradually access more advanced features.

Clear Visual Cues

The model for user behavior with a web app on a desktop or even mobile devices is mature. Users are accustomed to the functions associated with different elements and they understand input methods, such as click and right-click on desktops or swipe and pinch on touch-enabled mobile devices. Some of the same functions apply to UIs designed for Google TV, but the overall model is different.

As you'll find in Chapter 3, D-Pad navigation should be the primary way that users interact with your web app. This approach means that you should constrain the UI to reflect changes in state, selection, or focus based on left, right, up, or down navigation. Your UX should rely on clear visual cues that are explicit in giving a user a sense of what's selected or where a user has set the focus of the D-Pad. Your goal is to make it as easy and intuitive as possible for users to understand the context of their actions.

TV-friendly Navigation

Along with clear visual cues, a compelling app should enable users to easily navigate and select content. There are endless possibilities for setting up navigation flow around a site, so the idea is to eliminate the painful parts of navigation.

Providing users with access to content that is buried under six menu levels or forcing users to scroll through hundreds of entries may not be the best idea when a user is laying on his sofa and using the D-Pad to navigate around your content. Your goal is to get the user to the content they want as quickly as possible.

What You'll Need

Fortunately, building web apps for Google TV does not require some new custom language or an obscure SDK with limited frameworks. We're talking about the same tools that developers already use to build web apps for browsers on other devices. At your disposal are HTML, JavaScript, CSS, and Flash.

Of course, you'll also need some way to serve the content, and if you plan on doing this dynamically, you'll likely want to use a server side language like Ruby, PHP, or Java, as well as some data store like MySQL or CouchDB. We won't dive deep into any one of these languages (or even your web app's server-side architecture), but we will provide some pointers in case you need to come up to speed.

Background Knowledge

You'll need to have some knowledge beyond plain HTML, unless you plan on building a static web page that offers no interactivity. To build a good app, you'll want to use advanced HTML, JavaScript, and CSS, or Flash (or a combination thereof). Ideally, you've developed web apps that are compatible with modern browsers, such as Google Chrome or Safari. Don't worry if you don't have this experience, as fortunately there is a *lot* of information out there on web development.

 You may come across some reference documentation that discusses the need for "cross-browser compatibility." If you're developing generic websites that will be accessed on other devices, such as laptops, then you'll want to pay attention to cross-browser compatibility. Otherwise, you can get away with browser-specific design for the Chrome browser only.

There are numerous resources out there to get you up to speed on developing web apps. First and foremost, you'll want to familiarize yourself with the process of web development and the concept of a web app. Google's *http://code.google.com* is a good place to familiarize yourself with some of the technologies that we'll be using. If you're just starting out, it's worthwhile to check out a few websites before diving into books. Be sure to check out the following resources.

HMTL5

HTML5Rocks: *http://HTML5Rocks.com*

Dive into HTML5: *http://DiveIntoHTML5.org*

Apple's HTML5 Demos: *http://www.apple.com/html5/*

HTML5?

What exactly is HTML5? Is it a new feature or some sort of specification?

HTML5 is the next version of the HTML specification that is managed by the W3C (the main standards and specifications body for the web). And it's also a general term used to refer to the combined use of HTML, CSS, and JavaScript to produce web apps for web browsers that support the HTML5 specification. In essence "HTML5" is used as a general term to describe a combination of features that are available on "modern" browsers.

Flash

Adobe's Flash Developer Center: *http://www.adobe.com/devnet/flash.html*

Smashing Magazine: Flash Tutorials - Best Of: *http://www.smashingmagazine.com/2008/01/17/adobe-flash-tutorials-best-of/*

Flash Perfection (Flash tutorials): *http://www.flashperfection.com/*

Books

Once you've familiarized yourself with HTML5 and Flash, you'll want to dive a bit deeper into specific topics. Here are some good reference books that we think will give you some good, practical knowledge:

- *Head First HTML with CSS & XHTML (http://oreilly.com/catalog/9780596101978)*, First Edition, by Elisabeth Freeman and Eric Freeman (O'Reilly)
- *HTML5: Up and Running (http://oreilly.com/catalog/9780596806033)*, First Edition, by Mark Pilgrim (O'Reilly)
- *JavaScript: The Missing Manual (http://oreilly.com/catalog/9780596515898)*, First Edition, by David Sawyer McFarland (O'Reilly)
- *Learning Flash CS4 Professional: Getting Up to Speed with Flash (http://oreilly.com/catalog/9780596159757/)*, First Edition, by Rick Schupe (O'Reilly)
- *Flash CS5: The Missing Manual (http://oreilly.com/catalog/0636920000631)*, First Edition, by Chris Grover (O'Reilly)
- *Programming Google App Engine (http://oreilly.com/catalog/9780596522735)*, First Edition, by Dan Sanderson (O'Reilly)

 Note that to develop web apps using Flash you'll need to purchase and use a proprietary editor such as Adobe's Flash CS5. This tip is not meant to dissuade you from using Flash, which itself is very powerful and versatile, but we want to make you aware of the requirement in case you opt to go the Flash route.

Tools

Writing Code

We'd like to ensure that as wide an audience can follow along with the code in this book, so we've used a simple text editor to write and edit code. You may or may not be familiar with integrated development environments (IDEs), but many developers rely on these desktop applications to streamline their code development.

Our assumption is that if you already use an IDE, then you are technically savvy enough to adapt your coding workflow as needed. If you do not use an IDE, then we suggest that you use a source code text editor or explore using an IDE. This article provides a good overview of text editors and the various operating systems that support them:

http://goo.gl/mB6Sz (*http://en.wikipedia.org/wiki/Source_code_editor*)

Working with Images

As far as working with images, we'll leave it up to you to use your preferred image editing software. Making an aesthetically pleasing UI is important and you'll need image editing software to create "assets" such as icons, buttons, backgrounds, and other graphics. You'll also likely need image editing software to optimize or scale content, such as photographs or diagrams.

Applications like Adobe Photoshop are great, but they are not free. One popular free alternative is GIMP (GNU Image Manipulation Program), an open source image editing application that runs in most of the popular operating systems.[†]

As with source code editors, the following Wikipedia article on graphic art software has references to various types of image editing software that you will likely find useful:

http://goo.gl/BteWZ (*http://en.wikipedia.org/wiki/Graphic_art_software*)

If you don't have any image editing software currently installed, we suggest trying out one of the free open source apps to get started.

 If graphic design isn't your strength, you can use stock images available from various online vendors. Remember to only use images that you have the legal right to use and to evaluate the licensing terms attached to images available from online vendors.

Developing with Flash

If you plan on using Flash to develop a web app, you'll need an authoring tool to create the SWF (small wave format) files used by Google Chrome to access and render Flash on Google TV. Although there are some third party IDEs, Adobe's own Flash CS5 software is the most appropriate and relevant tool for you to build a Flash web app. Another alternative is to use image editing software, such as Adobe Photoshop or Adobe Fireworks, to export small animations to SWF format.

Note that Flash also can be used to stream video content. We'll cover that in a bit more detail in Chapter 6.

Hosting Web Apps

If you're just getting started, you'll also want to set up a web server to host your app. There are a variety of ways to host a web app: you can set up a site on a shared server,

---

† You can learn more about GIMP and download it at *http://www.gimp.org*.

use a dedicated server, or utilize cloud-based platforms that enable you to set up temporary or permanent virtualized servers.

The most popular and low-cost way to set up a server to host your web app is to use a shared server on one of the many hosting services out there. There are thousands (perhaps tens of thousands) of web hosting providers out there, but some of the more popular ones include Bluehost.com, Go Daddy, HostGator, Media Temple, and Rackspace.

Another option that we think is worth exploring is App Engine, Google's cloud-based platform, which provides a tiered price model for hosting web apps built with Python and Java. The base tier is free, and even if you're not a Python or Java developer, App Engine can be used to host static files, including HTML, JavaScript, and CSS. You can learn more at *http://appengine.google.com*.

Google's Resources

Google has several online resources that you'll find useful as you move forward with your development efforts. These resources are all primarily aimed at developers experienced with web development, so if you're just starting out, we encourage you to check out the resources we've listed in the preceding sections.

Google TV Code Site (http://code.google.com/tv/web)
> This site provides general guidance on some of the same topics covered in this book. Be sure to check out the implementation tips as well as the website optimization checklist.

Google TV Web Forum (https://groups.google.com/group/googletv-web)
> This forum is a great resource for developers to ask technical questions about Google TV web development. It's also a good venue to connect with other Google TV web developers.

Google TV Optimized Templates (http://code.google.com/tv/web/docs/gtv-templates .html)
> In early 2011, the Google TV team released a set of open source templates in both HTML5 and Flash. These templates serve as a good starting point for building a web app to serve video.

Google TV Web UI Libraries (http://code.google.com/tv/web/lib/)
> In addition to the optimized templates, the Google TV team released a set of JavaScript libraries that can be used in conjunction with the templates. One library is based on jQuery and another library is based on Google's Closure JavaScript framework.

The 10-Foot Experience

The last bit of wisdom we'd like to pass on before diving into a more technical discussion is some context for what is commonly referred to as the "lean-back" or 10-foot experience. Getting a grasp on this experience is not necessarily difficult, but it can be difficult to target your web apps for the 10-foot experience, especially if you're accustomed to developing web apps for desktops and laptops.

One of the inherent challenges is that you'll be developing your web app on a different device than Google TV. Yes, you can view and test your app on Google TV, but you'll be writing code, modifying images, and troubleshooting on your computer, among other devices. This can pose a challenge, as your initial interaction with a web app will be in the "2-foot experience." This is not a major issue, however, provided that you keep in mind the general context for the 10-foot experience.

Environment

We've already touched on the target environment a bit, but it's worth reiterating that your web app will be used in a casual environment, more than likely the living room. While this little bit of knowledge may seem trivial, we often see this aspect overlooked in many of the web apps developers have put together for TV. It is key for you to remember that your app will be used in the living room or an equivalent environment.

Mind-set

What's your attitude when you're in front of your TV? Do you feel high-strung or relaxed? Ideally it's the latter. Most people are in a relaxed mind-set when they're in front of their TV. Even if you're asking the user to interact with the TV or if your web app is more of a utility, it should still accommodate the mind-set that people have when they're used to relaxing ten feet away from a big screen.

Interaction

How have you traditionally interacted with your TV? This question will help you pinpoint how you should lead your users in terms of features and functionality, both of which drive user interaction. There are existing models that a majority of users have become accustomed to when it comes to interacting with their TVs. Consider how you currently interact with your TV and transfer that knowledge to your app.

CHAPTER 3

Designing the 10-Foot User Interface

In this chapter, we'll cover some of the common challenges that developers face when they go about designing a 10-foot user interface for web apps. Our goal is for you to gain a better understanding of the nuances between an application viewed from a distance versus one viewed nearby on your laptop or desktop computer.

Focus on Design First, Implementation Second

When developing your web app, it's always a good idea to break down the project into separate phases. As you may already know, the design phase is often the most critical and time consuming step in a project. Though you may want to quickly dive in and start implementing right away, you should fight this urge and focus on the design phase.

Jumping to the implementation phase before design mocks are created can often result in hours forfeited to developing an imperfect prototype. This can often limit your development in the following ways:

1. Constricts and limits design freedom based on your implementation
2. Potentially forces you to reject what you currently have, leading you to start from scratch

As you start to develop a 10-foot user interface, focus on design first. Set a goal to mock up anywhere from three to six interfaces, each posing a different perspective, then evaluate the pros and cons of each. Subsequently, evaluate, combine, and reiterate until you have a user interface with which you are happy.

Learn from Other 10-Foot User Experiences

There are already various 10-foot interfaces being used today on TV. The Google TV UI is one vision of a 10-foot user experience, but there are other UIs worth comparing as well. Figure 3-1 shows the home screen for XBMC, a media center operating system branched from Xbox.

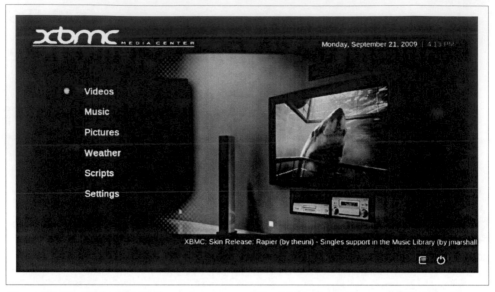

Figure 3-1. The UI for XBMC (formerly known as Xbox Media Center) is targeted for TV and serves as a nice example of a simple, streamlined UI

Notice that the UI displays both static and dynamic information. The navigation to browse different categories of content is positioned on the left, with a visual icon indicating where the current selection cursor exists. This interface requires the user to interact with it before presenting any data to the user. Figure 3-2 shows how the UI changes when a user elects to see her video library.

Figure 3-2. The view of a video library in XBMC

Notice the carousel viewing mechanism to browse videos based on a visual image. The item with a focused selection and highlighted border is the item currently selected. Its icon is also larger than the rest and centered, providing additional visual queues to the user about which item is currently selected. As you can see in Figure 3-3, the UI changes again when a user switches to a music library.

Figure 3-3. A music library UI, notice that the selection is not as easily discerned in this UI as it is with the video library

This music library is presented to the user in grid list format with vertical scrolling, and the current selection is identified this time only by a highlighted border.

While the scope of this book doesn't allow us to comprehensively cover all of the 10-foot UIs out there, some other UIs targeted for TV that may be worth a look before you embark on your own design include UIs used in multipurpose gaming consoles, such as XBOX 360 and PlayStation 3, as well as UIs from other TV devices, such as Boxee and Apple TV. Our goal is not to draw comparisons here, but rather for you to get a sense of and draw inspiration from the various approaches that exist.

 You can also read about 10-foot user interfaces on Wikipedia at *http://goo.gl/pp5pc*.

Fundamentals of the 10-Foot User Interface

Reference: User Interface Elements

We'll be referencing common phrases and objects throughout the chapter to denote a specific element or section of the interface. In order to reference these elements, they need to be clearly defined to the reader. Take a look at Figure 3-4, which displays various UI elements referenced throughout the chapter.

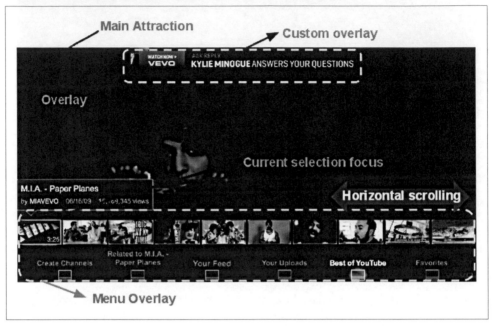

Figure 3-4. YouTube Leanback interface with various UI elements highlighted

Understand Your Users

As we discussed in Chapter 2, environment, mind-set, and interaction factor into a user's 10-foot experience. Although there is some variability around these factors, there are certain usability patterns which hold true for most, if not all, users.

Google TV is an open platform that connects a variety of users to web apps. To optimize this experience for users, it's important to understand that there is a spectrum of users that will use your web app.

On one end of the spectrum, there are "passive" users. These users relax on the sofa in a comfortable position, leaning back while casually surfing the web. They will perform basic web browsing actions, such as searching for videos, using a single hand and finger on the remote. Unnecessary movement is avoided and minimized in this case. The less energy spent swapping fingers and searching for the right buttons to push on the remote, the better. They generally don't care so much about what other capabilities or features an application has to offer.

Passive users typically exhibit the following characteristics:

- D-Pad navigation is vital
- Multimedia transport controls are a plus
- May quickly feel overwhelmed and confused by complex interfaces
- Rarely prefers to use mouse track pad and clicker
- Unlikely to discover or use shortcut keys
- Simple interface, interactions, and input devices are preferred

On the opposite end of the spectrum are "power" users. These users enjoy the challenge of learning how to do what they want, even if the user experience is less than optimal. Power users find the qwerty keyboard input device favorable, similar to their interactions with a personal computer. They are fully engaged and hardly inconvenienced by placing two hands on the input device in order to type more efficiently.

Power users may exhibit the following characteristics:

- D-Pad navigation is a plus, but not vital
- Prefers to use mouse trackpad and clicker
- Multimedia transport controls are rarely used
- Impressed by feature-rich applications and interfaces
- Appreciate complex input devices to provide more control
- Willing to discover, learn, and use shortcut keys

You may find that your application is geared more to one end of the spectrum than the other. Ultimately, how well your web app is used depends on the audience (as discussed in the previous chapter), so if you know that your audience is comprised of nontechnical users, your best bet is to design an app for passive users. Despite the versatility of power users, you should note that the D-Pad is relevant and relatively important for all users. In other words: D-Pad should be the primary means for interaction with your web apps.

Common Interface Elements

Within any user interface, there are a common set of interface elements, to which users respond differently depending on the context of their environment. Since we're designing 10-foot interfaces, common interface elements such as horizontal/vertical scrolling, layout, and overlays must behave differently in order to achieve the optimal user experience. There are important characteristics to remember for each element, including how each one may vary from traditional web browser designs.

Layout

The interface is comprised of many different elements, resulting in an almost infinite number of ways to choose a specific layout to present your content.

Figures 3-5 and 3-6 illustrate two common screen layouts which developers typically implement for Google TV. Figure 3-5 illustrates the "main attraction" approach, while Figure 3-6 illustrates the "embedded main attraction" approach. Both approaches have advantages and disadvantages, as we'll discuss.

Main Attraction

The main attraction layout is often used to display dynamic content, such as videos. Transparent menus are typically placed along one of the neighboring margins of the interface. Bottom or left margins are typically the most common. Note that additional overlays such as video playback controls and notification dialogs are generally placed in the middle where it's most visible and apparent to the user.

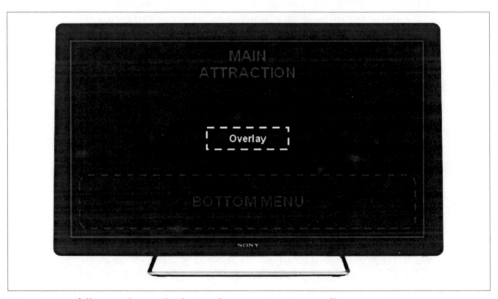

Figure 3-5. A full screen layout displaying the main attraction at all times

Advantages:

- Familiar interface from existing set-top box channel guide menus
- Main attraction is always visible and occupies the entire screen real estate
- Users can always hit "Esc" or "Exit" buttons to easily return to the main attraction
- Good for displaying video, sideshows, and live content
- Simple and user-friendly

Disadvantages:

- Not intuitive for content requiring more user input
- Menus and overlays may obstruct the view of the main attraction
- Generally limited to one-dimensional menus and submenus

Embedded Main Attraction

The main attraction layout typically displays a list of items in grid format or the live multimedia content itself in an embedded frame. This layout gives menus designated space on any side of the main attraction area, typically positioned to the left of it. Additional transparent overlays can sometimes be positioned over the main attraction area, but is not typically done if displaying static content such as a grid list of items.

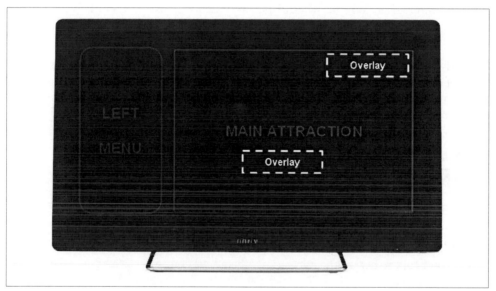

Figure 3-6. Note the difference in layout when using the embedded main attraction approach

Advantages:

- Good for presenting categories for users to browse through
- Persistent menus for presenting content via categories
- Good for static content and information like books and news

Disadvantages:

- Requires extra step to toggle main attraction to fullscreen mode
- Requires user interaction before loading content into main attraction area
- Interface is more complex with potentially lots of ways to navigate

Transparent Overlays

The following questions can help in determining whether to make any overlay transparent when displaying it over existing content:

1. Is the content behind the overlay displaying dynamic content such as streaming video?
2. Is there information behind the overlay which is important to remain visible to the user?
3. Is the overlay something which should display only temporarily and can be dismissed either by the user or via timer?

Note that not all overlays need to be transparent. Transparency generally indicates to the user that an overlay is merely a temporary layer placed above a more important piece of content. For example, when displaying video, it's best to make playback control overlays transparent so the user can see what's behind it, and also to indicate that it can be dismissed.

Similarly, when an overlay is opaque, it indicates to the user that a more important piece of data is contained within. For example, if the left menu column was displayed in opaque fashion, it would indicate the menu is persistent and cannot be dismissed, which may or may not always be true.

 Use transparency wisely. Overlays that are less important and configured to be dismissed either by a user or timer should be made transparent. The overlays for containers that are persistent and contain important data for the user to interact with should be made opaque.

Navigation

When you begin to design the navigation scheme for your interface, it may seem overwhelming at first, given all of the design considerations. The rule of thumb and preferred mode of navigating 10-foot interfaces is via keyboard navigation. All Google TV devices come equipped with an input device, including a D-Pad (Figure 3-7). Though a qwerty keyboard and trackpad are also available, all existing TV menus and interfaces today are generally designed to be interfaced with using a simple remote with a D-Pad. So we can't reiterate enough how important it is that your app use the D-Pad as the primary mechanism for navigation.

We'll touch more on this topic in the next two chapters, particularly Chapter 5, which dives deep into how to actually make a web app D-Pad navigable.

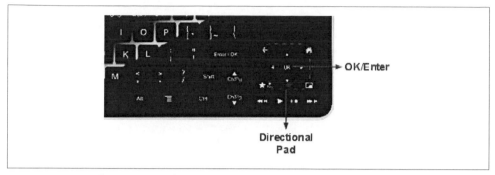

Figure 3-7. *Logitech Revue input device and its directional pad to navigate Google TV*

Scrolling

Traditional scrolling models which work well on desktop browsers do not translate well over to the 10-foot interface. Scrolling through traditional scroll bars with a D-Pad is not an optimal experience for users.

In almost all cases, design your own scrolling mechanism using animations to transition between items or pages smoothly. It's best to let the user's current selection initiate the scrolls as it moves across each item instead of supplying "next" or "previous" page links.

Figure 3-8 displays an example of a web application implementing horizontal scrolling. Notice that there are no page links for users to click on. Instead, the user simply navigates left or right using the directional pad to browse across the pages of the video gallery.

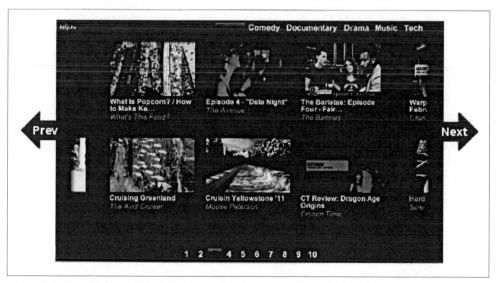

Figure 3-8. *The Blip.tv 10-foot interface uses horizontal scrolling based on the user's current selection*

The same scrolling mechanism can apply vertically. However, since TV screens are landscape with a wider width than height, there is considerably more screen real estate in the horizontal plane than there is in the vertical. If you need to implement scrolling in your interface, default to horizontal scrolling mechanisms whenever possible.

Typefaces and Graphics

Font sizes and graphics need to be large enough to be viewed comfortably from at least 10 feet away.

One tricky "gotcha" to setting typefaces and graphics is to take into account the two different resolutions in most HD displays. Depending on whether the viewer's display is rendering 1280 × 720 (720P) or 1920 × 1080 (1080P) resolutions, you may need to adjust your font and graphic sizes accordingly.

 Different fonts can add to the look and feel of your interface. Be sure to scroll through the list of fonts in the Google Font Directory at *http://code .google.com/webfonts* to get an idea of how custom fonts can be used in your web app.

Text

When designing a 10-foot interface, displaying less information is really key to driving a positive user experience. TV viewers will easily feel overwhelmed by text-heavy interfaces with complicated navigation schemes, menus, and buttons. If you're displaying text, consider trimming the text to only show a small snippet of it. A good rule of thumb is to use text the same way that you would in an art museum: you wouldn't expect visitors to read through more than a small description for a visual piece of art.

Visual and Audio Cues

Visual graphics and cues are a valuable way to keep users informed about navigation or state in a given application. Well-placed and well-timed visuals can dramatically improve the user experience and make the user feel more connected to the application. Text is often times cumbersome, takes up precious screen real estate, and does a poor job of communicating status to users. On the other hand, a well-done visual graphic, logo, or effect will not only improve the visual quality and polish of your application, but will also better convey what the application is doing behind the scenes.

One visual cue which you'll indefinitely need to design is the user's current selection focus (Figure 3-9). Users will rely on the selection focus to navigate and interact with your application, and thus you should aim to include the following logic:

- Only one selection focus exists
- Selection focus must be persistent and remain visible at all times
- Selection focus is driven by the D-pad

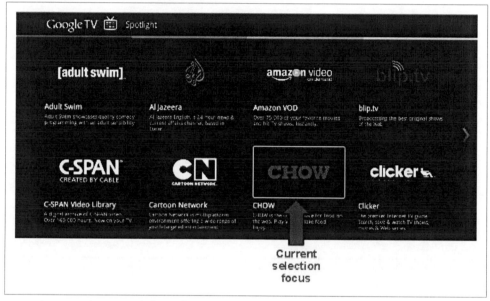

Figure 3-9. Google TV Spotlight 10-foot interface with single user selection focus

Audio cues can help liven up your app to give a much more polished feel. Playing a *subtle* sound effect each time the selection focus moves or behind toggling of a menu confirms to the user that her action was received. If you do decide to add audio effects and cues to your application, remember to include a way for users to toggle this functionality on or off. Google TV users may be watching another program or listening to music in the background as they explore and interact with your application, so the capability to disable sound is a requirement if you plan on including audio cues.

CHAPTER 4

Coding for the Leanback UI

Working with the Google Chrome Browser on a TV Display

Window Size and Overscan

How Overscan Impacts Design

As we've discussed previously, TV resolution on Google TV will be either 1080p or 720p. Content is broadcast expecting the legacy display characteristics of tube TVs, such as *overscan*, which in a tube TV represents the left and right side of a display where the image cannot be accurately displayed. Subsequently, content is clipped with the expectation that the left and right sides will not be displayed to the viewer. In digital displays, content is clipped by presenting less than the full number of pixels on the left and right side. Subsequently, to maintain the correct aspect ratio, the vertical resolution is also clipped.

When Google TV users initially adjust the display using the setup wizard, they're identifying the actual number of pixels visible on their TV display. For most TVs, this will be less than the display's ideal resolution and it also will vary based on models and brand.

Dealing with Ovescan

In designing pages for Google TV, taking overscan into account means that the resolution of the display, whether fundamentally 1080p or 720p, is never the same between TVs. There are two basic approaches a designer can take to accomodate overscan:

- A fixed-size page design, using elements of fixed size always fit onto a page assuming a 10% empty space around the page to account for overscan variability
- An adjustable page design (also known as a "fluid" layout) with elements that adjust to the page size or float on the page, moving to accommodate its dimensions

Fixed Page Design. You'll discover that a fixed page design may result in a large amount of empty space on the right and bottom edges of the screen for displays that are close to full resolution. You can mitigate this issue somewhat by detecting the real size of the window and moving the top-left corner down and to the right so that the empty space is even on all sides.

This design has a number of advantages: content can be a fixed, predictable size, and the visual appearance of the page will be predictable and conform to your original design intent. However, one disadvantage is that you may need two sets of designs for 1080p and 720p resolutions (unless the content and layout scales well; see "Autozoom Considerations" on page 42 for more details).

Adjustable Page Design. An adjustable design usually allows for a single page to serve both 1080p and 720p resolutions, and all variations of overscan for those displays. Floating the components on the page allows for additional flexibility.

The primary disadvantage of this design is that it may require considerably more effort to have one design and one set of content adjust and float across many different displays. For floating designs, D-pad navigation becomes more difficult to make intuitive because the relative positions of elements on the page can change for different display sizes.

Webkit Extensions for HTML5

The Google Chrome browser in Google TV benefits from a number of webkit extensions for CSS3. Since websites built for Google TV can rely on these extensions being available for their site, you can use these extensions to create compelling, dedicated 10-foot user experiences.

These extensions provide enhancements to the visual appeal of a page, including drop shadows and rounded corners on boxes, as well as "cinematic" effects using transitions and animations of CSS properties like position, rotation, size, color, opacity, and so on.

We'll touch on most of the relevant webkit extensions later in this chapter.

Google TV's User Agent String

Google TV includes a specific user agent string that is sent in the browser's request headers. This user agent string ideally should be used to serve the appropriate and relevant content to the Chrome browser on Google TV, including web apps created for Google TV or "TV-friendly" versions of your web app.

Here are the high-level steps to implement this behavior for Google TV users:

1. Detect the Google TV user-agent string by looking for the sub-strings *Large Screen* and *GoogleTV*, instead of trying to match the entire string. Here's an example of a recent user-agent string:

   ```
   Mozilla/5.0 (X11; U; Linux i686; en-US) AppleWebKit/533.4
   (KHTML, like Gecko) Chrome/5.0.375.127
   Large Screen Safari/533.4 GoogleTV/161242
   ```

2. Perform one of two options depending on whether you're using an adapted site or a web app catered for Google TV:

   - Display the TV-friendly version of your site (based on CSS and HTML changes)
   - Redirect (temporary 302) to your web app

Migrating an Existing Website

Websites designed to be accessed on browsers in desktop or laptop computers generally require a few essential changes to provide a decent user experience in a 10-foot environment.

Traditional page designs are built for a window in portrait dimensions, navigated with a mouse pointer, and rely on vertical scrolling provided by the browser window to reach additional content on the page. This type of design contrasts with the types of designs we covered in the previous chapter.

Adding Keyboard Navigation

Keyboard navigation is one of the most essential components of the user experience in a 10-foot interface. Although adding an event handler to handle key down events for arrow keys is essential for keyboard navigation, it is not the only element to consider.

Ideally, *every actionable element* on a page should be reachable using the D-pad arrow keys. These elements should be visually highlighted as the user navigates around them to make it clear where they are on the page. Once an element is highlighted, the user should be able to trigger it with the OK or ENTER keys.

If the page has logical groupings of controls, it's helpful to group the navigation as well. That is, allowing the highlight to "jump" around to disparate parts of the page can be confusing. An implementation can control for this by grouping the elements that can be highlighted by the containers that hold them. A keypress, such as the TAB key, can then be used to jump between areas of the page that would otherwise contain the highlight movement.

Autozoom Considerations

The Chrome browser on Google TV includes an algorithm for automatically zooming into page content. This *autozoom* is used to provide a basic level of usability for sites that were not designed for Google TV. By zooming in or out, the size of fonts and images is increased to a minimum readable size.

A website that requires autozoom for basic usability does not present an optimal user experience. Sites that have been designed for Google TV can still make use of autozoom to improve the user experience while saving effort. Using autozoom this way may degrade website display performance (such as with animations and scrolling), but this may be offset by the work for your design (and development) for multiple resolutions and for different TV overscan dimensions.

If you want to design your site without having to compensate for autozoom, you can disable this feature with the following `meta` tag:

```
<meta name="gtv-autozoom" content="off" />
```

Scrolling and Paging Content

Traditional web pages use scroll bars automatically provided by the browser to scroll through content. These scroll bars might be on the main browser window or in individual elements (for example, DIVs with the CSS property `overflow: scroll` set).

The 10-foot user experience makes it difficult for users to select a relatively small scroll bar on the display and position it accurately. Given this limitation, it's better to rely on D-pad arrow keys to scroll a page instead and navigate individual items. In short, you shouldn't rely on scroll bars to access off-screen content, as this will likely punish your users with a relatively poor experience.

Content Sizing for Fonts and Images

Reading from a display at a 10-foot distance requires fonts that are significantly larger than traditional pages. As a general rule of thumb, fonts should be a minimum of 16pt for 720p displays and 20pt for 1080p displays.

Images should be scaled to have the same visual impact at 10 feet. Note that the scale factor is not linear with the size of the display and the viewer's distance. In technical terms, this is because the angle of view that a pixel of a certain size covers does not vary linearly with the viewer's distance from the screen.

 Since bitmap image content does not scale up losslessly, if one set of images is used for both 1080p and 720p, the best approach is to choose 1080p images and scale them down to the appropriate size.

Although not necessarily recommended, a simple approach to scaling all content is to use the CSS zoom property to scale the page. This property can be applied to the `<body>` element to scale all of the child elements proportionately. The number used for this property should be fixed, not calculated, and selected to be a factor of 2 or 1/2 for scaling efficiency where possible.

Working with HTML5

Audio and Video

HTML5 provides native support for audio and video playback with the `<audio>` and `<video>` tags.

In most cases, playback will also mean providing media key support as well as D-pad navigable controls for play, pause, fast-forward, and rewind.

These media types have `play` and `pause` methods to control playback, and you can simulate fast-forward and rewind by changing the currentTime of the element in small increments up or down. The following code snipped shows a key handler that handles fast-forward, rewind, and play/pause keys to control video playback:

```
var video = createElement('video');
// ...
window.addEventListener('keydown', function(e) {
  switch e.keyCode {
    case 227:
      // fast forward 10 seconds
      video.currentTime += 10;
      break;
    case 228:
      // rewind 10 seconds
      video.currentTime -= 10;
      break;
    case 179:
      if (video.paused) {
        video.play();
      } else {
        video.pause();
      }
  }
});
```

CSS3 Flexible Box Model

The CSS3 *Flexible Box* model (also known simply as FlexBox) provides an easy way to fit content into a container `<div>`. Child elements of the container can be spaced out horizontally or vertically, stretched to fit the container, and given a relative size ratio to assist the browser in spacing the child elements. Instead of having to fiddle with floating elements or percentage sizes, each of which cause other complexities with design, you can use a flexible box container to handle all of this automatically with a few properties.

You can learn more about the Flexible Box Model at:

W3 Consortium's Flexible Box Module: *http://goo.gl/UXEzY*

HTML5Rocks.com offers an introductory article on the Flexible Box Model: *http://goo.gl/Xgoh*

We won't cover all of the details of the flexible box model, but instead will focus on the more relevant concepts and properties.

display: -webkit-box

This property enables the flexible box model in a container. Children of this container will be laid out according to their flexible box properties when they are added to an enabled parent.

-webkit-box-orient

This property, set on the container element, can be either `horizontal` or `vertical`. Child elements will be sized to fit in the axis specified.

-webkit-box-flex

This property, set on the child elements, specifies the fraction of space a child will occupy in its container relative to its siblings. For example, if a box has two elements and one specifies `-webkit-box-flex: 1` and the other specifies `-webkit-box-flex: 3`, then the second element will occupy three times the space in the box as its sibling.

Relevant CSS3 Properties

Animations and Transitions

JavaScript libraries like jQuery provide abstractions for providing animations and transitions of elements on the page. These commonly allow the *translation* (movement of the element's origin on the page) and *transformation* (change in the element's dimensions) of elements on the page over time, along with a means for triggering an event when complete.

CSS3 provides its own means for animations and transitions of elements, as well as events triggered upon completion. Google Chrome generally supports these CSS3 features, but requires the `-webkit-` extension to signify a specific implementation of a still-evolving standard.

-webkit-transition. When this style is applied to an element, it signifies that style changes applied subsequently will transition from the initial state to the new state over time. This can be accomplished without any JavaScript code.

For example, the following page shows a green box that changes to a larger, red box when hovered over with the mouse:

```html
<html>
  <head>
    <style>
      body {
        overflow: hidden;
      }
      .wkt-demo {
        -webkit-transition-property: background-color, width, height;
        -webkit-transition-duration: 1s, 2s, 4s;
        -webkit-transition-timing-function: ease-in-out;
        -webkit-transition-delay: .25s;
      }
      .test-div {
        width: 50px;
        height: 50px;
        background-color: #0e0;
      }
      .test-div:hover {
        width: 300px;
        height: 300px;
        background-color: #e00;
      }
    </style>
  </head>
  <body>
    <div>
      <p>
        The DIV below will change background color, top and left positions
        using a CSS3 transition when hovered over, but each will change at
        a different rate.
      </p>
      <div class="test-div wkt-demo"></div>
    </div>
  </body>
</html>
```

webkitTransitionEnd event. A page could trigger JavaScript code at the completion of a transition. This could be used for additional animations or for activity to happen on the page when the transition is over, or merely to know that the transition has completed so that new events can be processed.

The webkitTransitionEnd event will fire when a transition completes successfully. If multiple transitions are timed (as in the previous example), multiple end events will be fired. The name of the property whose transition has ended is in the event's property Name attribute.

The new <body> contains the code that will add the property name to the page each time its transition ends:

```
<body>
  <script type="text/javascript">
    window.addEventListener('load', function() {
      var testDiv = document.getElementById('test');
      testDiv.addEventListener('webkitTransitionEnd', function(e) {
        var complete = document.getElementById('complete');
          complete.innerHTML += ' ' + e.propertyName;
        });
      });
  </script>
  <div>
    <p>
      The DIV below will change background color, top and left positions
      using a CSS3 transition, but each will change at a different rate.
    </p>
    <div>
      <p>
        Completed: <span id="complete"></span>
      </p>
    </div>
    <div id="test" class="test-div wkt-demo"></div>
  </div>
</body>
```

-webkit-animation. CSS3 animations provide another way to apply timed transitions of CSS properties to elements. Animations have the same related attributes as transitions. For example, -webkit-animation-delay represents the delay, in seconds, before an animation should begin once triggered.

What makes -webkit-animation different is that, where -webkit-transform continues to act on style changes to an element as long as it is present, -webkit-animation provides the ability to define a more complex movement using *keyframes*. Each keyframe is expressed as a percent of the total animation completion time, and every keyframe definition has a *from* and *to* frame that defines the start and end state for the element in the animation.

You can also loop animations a specific number of times or infinitely.

```
<html>
  <head>
    <style>
      body {
        overflow: hidden;
      }
      @-webkit-keyframes test-anim {
        from {
          width: 50px;
          height: 50px;
          background-color: #0e0;
        }
        50% {
```

```
            width: 600px;
            height: 600px;
            background-color: #00e;
        }
        to {
            width: 300px;
            height: 300px;
            background-color: #e00;
        }
    }
    .wkt-demo {
        -webkit-animation-name: test-anim;
        -webkit-animation-duration: 4s;
        -webkit-animation-timing-function: ease-in-out;
        -webkit-animation-iteration-count: infinite;
    }
    .test-div {
    }
    </style>
</head>
<body>
    <div>
        <p>
            The DIV below will change background color,
            width, and height using a CSS3 animation.
            At the start, the DIV is small and green;
            halfway through it is large and blue;
            at the end it is medium and red.
        </p>
        <div id="test" class="test-div wkt-demo"></div>
    </div>
</body>
</html>
```

webkitAnimationEnd event. This is similar to the webkitTransitionEnd event. You can listen for this event when using -webkit-animation- on your page.

-webkit-transform. The webkit-transform CSS3 style opens up a range of possibilities for cinematic effects on a Google TV web app when combined with transitions or animations. The webkit-transform style compounds a number of possible transforms into one attribute. Transforms available include *rotate* (X, Y, Z), *translate* (X, Y, Z), and *scale* (X, Y).

This animation rotates an element in all three dimensions, while scaling up the size of the element:

```
@-webkit-keyframes test-anim {
    from {
        -webkit-transform: rotate(0deg) rotateY(0deg) rotateZ(0deg);
    }
    to {
        -webkit-transform: rotateX(90deg) rotateY(270deg) rotateZ(45deg) scaleX(4)
        scaleY(8);
    }
}
```

Presentation Enhancements

-webkit-box-shadow. The box-shadow style allows a variety of shadow and outline effects around elements on a page. In its most basic form, the property takes just a horizontal and vertical offset from the element being styled:

```
-webkit-box-shadow: 5px, 5px;
```

The shadow can also be given a color, in this case green:

```
-webkit-box-shadow: 5px, 5px, #0e0;
```

Additional variants allow a blur distance and shadow spread, which can be used to give the drop shadow a softer edge or larger shadow:

```
-webkit-box-shadow: 5px, 5px, 3px, 4px #0e0;
```

An inset shadow draws the shadow inside the padding box of the element:

```
-webkit-box-shadow: inset 5px, 5px, 3px, 4px #0e0;
```

border-radius. The `border-radius` property is a popular CSS3 addition that provides rounded border corners. The corner is described in terms of the horizontal and vertical radii of a quarter eclipse. The easiest way to use the property is to have these be the same for all four corners:

```
border-radius: 10px;
```

However, it is possible to supply different radii for the horizontal and vertical portion of the corner:

```
border-radius: 10px / 5px;
```

Finally, if desired, each corner can have its own radius:

```
border-radius: 10px 7px 10px 7px;
border-radius: 10px 7px 10px 7px / 5px 2px 5px 2px;
```

Thus far, we've covered some of the core technical elements, including CSS3, that you should consider using for your web app. Obviously, if you are building your web app in Flash, you'll need to adapt some of the aforementioned logic and you won't rely on CSS3 transformations. Regardless of which development approach you take, the key is to understand that your web app needs to accomodate overscan and compensate for the issues that this may cause for elements in your UI. At the same time, designing a modern UI for your web app can be accomplished with fewer lines of code and a lesser reliance on images, if you utilize relevant CSS3 properties.

We'll take a deeper dive into the technical discussion around navigation, controls, and interactivity in the next chapter.

CHAPTER 5

Developing Your Web App

Putting a UI Together

Navigation

Using arrow keys or a D-pad for navigation is an essential part of the Google TV 10-foot experience. While it may seem straightforward at first, it can be complex to implement effective and flexible D-pad navigation for a web page. We'll start with a simple example of a regular grid of fixed navigable items, add a lefthand navigation bar, and then items along the top of the page for meta-tasks like login.

 You can use straight up JavaScript to code a web app, but we've found that the jQuery library enables effective and efficient JavaScript coding that can significantly reduce development time. You can learn more about jQuery at *http://jquery.com*.

A Regular Grid

Navigating a central section of a page with the arrow keys, which may be a regular grid (Figure 5-1), can be as simple as moving between adjacent items (left/right) and adjacent rows (up/down).

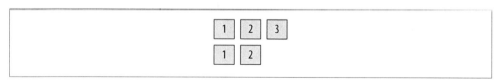

Figure 5-1. A regular grid layout for navigation, the most basic of designs

For flexibility, we'll define our content as follows:

```
<div class="container">
  <div class="item-row">
    <div class="item-div">
      <p class="item"></p>
    </div>
    <div class="item-div">
      <p class="item"></p>
    </div>
    <div class="item-div">
      <p class="item"></p>
    </div>
  </div>
  <div class="item-row">
    <div class="item-div">
      <p class="item"></p>
    </div>
    <div class="item-div">
      <p class="item"></p>
    </div>
  </div>
</div>
```

The items we select are of class item held in their columns by parents item-div, which are in turn held in rows by their item-row class parents.

In jQuery, we can set the selection to the first item in the grid with:

```
var selected = $.find('.item').first();
```

If the user presses the right arrow key, we can move to the item to the right by going to the next element of class item-div in the row:

```
var newSelected = selected.parent().next('.item-div').find('.item');
```

Note that we don't want to immediately overwrite selected with this next item. If we're at the rightmost item-div in the row, then newSelected here will select zero elements in the DOM. We check that case:

```
if (newSelected.length != 0)
  moveSelection(newSelected);
```

The moveSelected function here will remove the CSS class that highlights the item from the old selected item, add it to the newly selected item, and then set the selection.

```
function moveSelected(newSelected) {
  if (selected) {
    selected.removeClass('highlight');
  }
  newSelected.addClass('highlight');
}
```

If the user presses the down arrow, we want to select the item on the row below. We'll assume for now that we want to remain in the same column (that is, move vertically only, not return to the first item in the row). This means we need to find the item-div in the next row in the same vertical position. There are a number of ways to accomplish this: we can perform a search of the next row using the extents of the item on the page, we can keep track of our index into the row, or we can attach a column number to each item in the row representing the column number.

For now, we'll assume that we've used jQuery.data() to attach a column number to each item. We'll iterate over each row and then over each item in the row, assigning index numbers:

```
$.find('item-row').each(function() {
  $(this).find('.item').each(function(index) {
    $(this).data('index', index);
  }
}
```

Now we can move to the next row:

```
var newSelected;
var selectedIndex = selected.data('index');
var nextRow = selected.parents('.item-row').next();
if (nextRow.length) {
  while (selectedIndex >= 0 && (!newSelected || newSelected.length == 0)) {
    newSelected = nextRow.find('.item-div').eq(selectedIndex).find('.item');
    selectedIndex -= 1;
  }
}
if (newSelected && newSelected.length > 0)
  moveSelected(newSelected);
```

Notice that we use a loop to select the next item in the row below. It's possible that the next row has fewer items in it. For example, if we're on index 2 (third item) on the first row, and we move down to the second row, which has only two items, we want the selection to "snap" to the second item.

Now we have to call this code from our "keydown" event listener, using logic like this:

```
$(document).bind('keydown', function(e) {
  switch e.keyCode {
    case 37:  // left
      break;
    case 38:  // up
      break;
    case 39:  // right
      break;
    case 40:  // down
      break;
  }
});
```

This code (plus handling for left and up, which are mirror operations of right and down) will allow the user to navigate around a grid of items on a page. A good way to start to do this is to add a key code listener for the ENTER key (which has key code 13), and then handle the keydown event on this key as if the user had clicked on that item.

But we want our users to be able to access every *clickable* control on the page with our keyboard navigation code; unless the only thing we have on our page is a set of items arranged in a grid, we have more work to do. We want our users to be able to move other parts of the page, such as to a left navigation pane or to a login button on the page header.

Nearest Neighbor Navigation

This code relies on having the elements on the page indexed so that it can maintain the column position when navigating between rows. However, we might also choose to look through items in the DOM, calculate their position and distance from the current item and, taking into account the direction of movement, choose the next nearest item to select.

This approach has advantages: it doesn't require us to index the items, and if the items float around the page into different positions, our navigation code still works because it depends on the actual position of the element instead of its "expected" position in a row and column.

There are disadvantages as well: when moving between elements of different sizes, going back and forth between them might not produce repeatable results. For instance, in the layout in Figure 5-2, A is the selected item. Pressing the right arrow will choose "C" (Figure 5-3) because it is the nearest element to the right. And then pressing the left arrow will choose "B" (Figure 5-4) because it is the nearest element to the left.

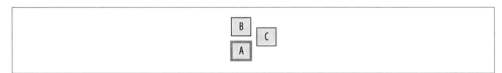

Figure 5-2. A is initially select, until the user presses the right arrow

Figure 5-3. C is the only element on the right side

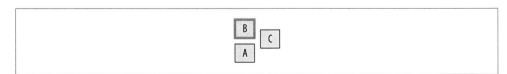

Figure 5-4. Pressing the left arrow does not return to A, but rather to B, which is in closer spatial proximity

The algorithm for finding the nearest element starts by selecting all items in the container with the `.item` class. Then it iterates through each item (skipping the selected item), looking for the item with the shortest Euclidean distance from the selected item.

Mouse and Keyboard

While many users will move the selection around with only the keyboard, many will use the mouse or a combination of the two.

The best way to handle this is to implement a `mouseenter` event listener on every selectable item and move the selection to the item when its entered:

```
var items = $.find('.item');
items.bind('mouseenter', function() {
  moveSelected($(this));
}
```

Similarly, you'll want to bind the `click` event to these items such that pressing enter and clicking perform the same action.

Full-Page Navigation

Full-page navigation requires that one selection be maintained across the entire page so that it's clear to the user what action would be taken were they to press OK or ENTER.

This sort of behavior can be easy to accomplish on pages with few controls. In most designs, however, a page often naturally segments into multiple logical sections. For instance, a page might have a menu on the side allowing the user to navigate to different areas of a site. The center of the page contains the main navigable content. Across the top of the page might be buttons for user login, settings, etc.

Segmented Pages

It's often convenient to segment these parts of the page into separate objects to encapsulate the functionality, as is generally the case for pages populated with reusable UI components.

Having each component manage keyboard input events and navigation between its elements is still possible, although this approach results in several handlers being called for every key and mouse event they manage, and that behavior can cause performance problems if not coded carefully.

More critically, if the controls handle navigation independently, they still need a way to make sure that there is only one highlighted item on the page. This would require a hand-off protocol for the selection between the controls, which can quickly become complicated.

Unified Navigation

A unified navigation system for the page is an approach that can address this problem. It has the benefit of being able to own the highlight for the page, and avoids having each control handling a hand-off protocol or becoming complicated with common navigation tasks and event handling.

For a unified controller to work, each control has be registered with it. Controls designed with unified system in mind can participate directly. However, reusing existing controls requires a system that can register controls on their behalf.

One approach to this is to create a key navigation system that treats all page elements in a particular container (e.g., a DIV) as part of a control, and recognizes items in that container with a CSS class as participating in the navigation system.

Input Controls

Input controls, such as text input boxes, present specific challenges to key navigation. When on a page, the user needs to be able to navigate to these controls and give them focus (for example, by moving the highlight to them and pressing OK or ENTER). Once these controls have focus, the user has to be able to navigate within the control, perhaps using the left and right arrows to move the cursor inside a text input box. This has to happen without the highlight moving to other elements of the page. Finally, the user needs to be able to use the keyboard to blur the control and resume moving the highlight to other elements of the page.

Handling Special Keys

The Google TV keyboard contains a few keys that are prominent in the everyday browsing experience of the user. These include the media keys (play, pause, fast-forward, rewind, skip forward, skip back) and the back key.

Media Keys

The media keys are prominently placed on the Google TV controllers, and users will naturally expect these keys to be functional while watching video or listening to music in the 10-foot environment. Implementing support for these keys is a matter of configuring an onkeydown event handler.

```
window.addEventListener('keydown', function(e) {
  switch e.keyCode {
    case 176:
      // Skip forward
      break;
    case 177:
      // Skip back
      break;
    case 178:
      // Stop
```

```
        break;
    case 179:
      // Play/Pause
      break;
    case 227:
      // Fast forward
      break;
    case 228:
      // Rewind
      break;
  }
});
```

The Back Key

In the Chrome browser on Google TV, the back key is interpreted as a page navigation to the previous page in the browsing history. As such, the browser does not pass on the key press, so it is not captured by any JavaScript key events.

For websites that change state by using script to manipulate the DOM instead of browsing to distinct page URLs, this presents a challenge. Since these sites don't automatically generate any browser history when their state changes, browsing to the previous URL in the user's history would result in her leaving the site; worse, if the site is the only entry in her history, she would be returned to the Google TV home page.

This issue can be addressed by using the hash component of the browser location. This approach is not difficult, and is used by many non-Google TV sites that face this challenge.

The mechanics of the approach are simplified by the addition, in HTML5, of the on-hashchange event, which is fired whenever the hash part of the location changes. (Previously, detecting the hash change required a timed polling loop.)

The following code implements a simple page that adds to the browser history by adding a location hash as the state changes. It then handles the onhashchange event and uses it to return the page to the appropriate state. Figure 5-5 illustrates how the first page in the following code example will render.

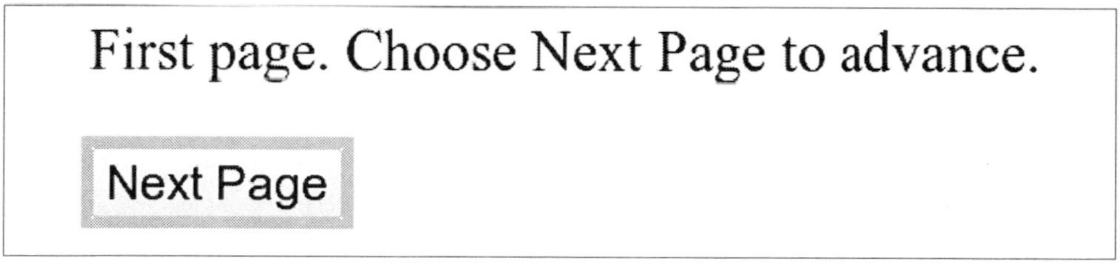

Figure 5-5. The first page of the back-key handling sample

```html
<html>
  <head>
    <style type="text/css">
      #page {
        -webkit-transition: opacity 1s ease-out;
        font-size: 24pt;
      }
      #next {
        visibility: hidden;
        outline: 6px solid #0e0;
        font-size: 20pt;
      }
    </style>
    <script type="text/javascript">
      var states = [
        'First page. Choose Next Page to advance.',
        'Second page. You can go on from here, or press the back key.',
        'Last page. Use the back key to go back.'
      ];

      var currentPage = 0;

      window.addEventListener('load', function() {
        // Handle the ENTER key and click event on the Next Page button.
        window.addEventListener('keydown', function(e) {
          // ENTER key
          if (e.keyCode == '13') {
            handleNext(e);
          }
        });
        var nextButton = document.getElementById('next');
        nextButton.addEventListener('click', handleNext);

        // Add a listener function to be called when the opacity fade
        // transition on the page element completes.
        var pagePara = document.getElementById('page');
        pagePara.addEventListener('webkitTransitionEnd', textFadeDone);

        // Add the all-important hashchange event to tell us when the user
        // pressed the back key.
        window.addEventListener('hashchange', handleBack);


        showPage(0);
      });

      function handleNext() {
        showPage(currentPage + 1);
      }

      function handleBack() {
        // Parse the hash string for the page number
        var newPage = parseInt(location.hash.substring(1)) || 0;
        if (newPage == currentPage) {
          // If the hash page matches the current page, just return.
```

```
          // This prevents showPage from being called recursively when we
          // change the hash.
          return;
        }
        showPage(newPage);
      }

      function textFadeDone() {
        var pagePara = document.getElementById('page');
        pagePara.innerHTML = states[currentPage];
        pagePara.style.opacity = 1;

        var nextButton = document.getElementById('next');
        if (currentPage < states.length - 1) {
          nextButton.style.visibility = 'visible';
        }
      }

      function showPage(newPage) {
        if (newPage < 0 || newPage >= states.length) {
          return;
        }
        currentPage = newPage;

        var pagePara = document.getElementById('page');
        pagePara.style.opacity = 0;

        var nextButton = document.getElementById('next');
        if (currentPage == states.length - 1) {
          nextButton.style.visibility = 'hidden';
        }

        if (currentPage) {
          location.hash = currentPage + '';
        } else {
          location.hash = '';
        }
      }

    </script>
  </head>
  <body>
    <div>
      <p id="page"></p>
      <button id-"next" type="button">Next Page</button>
    </div>
  </body>
</html>
```

Controls

We'll use the term "controls" to refer to any collection of elements under a common container that act together to provide a particular user experience. Controls often are encapsulated, reusable components and may be entirely from declarative HTML5/CSS3, entirely created at runtime in script, or some combination of the two.

This section discusses several control types that are common to 10-foot UI design and provides some sample implementations in HTML5/CSS3/JavaScript. The same logic can be adapted for Flash and Actionscript.

Menu Bars

For most pages on a 10-foot UI, the content is the star of the show. Even so, the user needs a way to navigate around the site, access different content, change settings, and interact with the web app.

A common design approach to accomodate this need is the use of a navigation bar on the page. The navigation bar might contain thumbnails, descriptions of categories or subsections, or other appropriate filters. The user needs to be able reach the menu bar using the D-pad, choose an item, and then move back to the content.

The following sample code builds a static left-side menu (Figure 5-6) that can be navigated with the D-pad. This sample uses the CSS3 Flexible Box to arrange the menu items vertically on the page. It automatically positions and scales the child elements, considerably simplifying the CSS required to describe the menu.

```html
<html>
  <head>
    <style type="text/css">
      html, body {
        height: 100%;
        overflow: hidden;
      }
      div.scroll-container > div {
        -webkit-box-flex: 1;
        background-color: #333;
        color: #eee;
        font-size: 20pt;
        margin: 5px;
        padding: 5px;
        border: 5px solid #999;
        border-radius: 15px;
      }
      div.scroll-container {
        display: -webkit-box;
        -webkit-box-orient: vertical;
        float: left;
        position: relative;
        height: 80%;
        width: 25%;
```

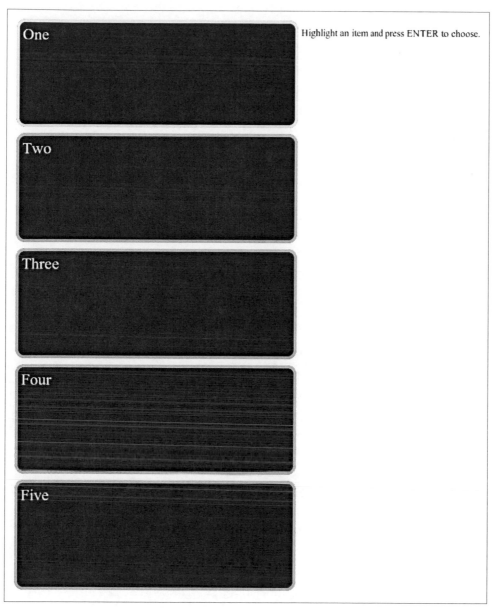

One

Two

Three

Four

Five

Highlight an item and press ENTER to choose.

Figure 5-6. A left-side navigation menu

```
}
.item-highlight {
  border-color: #ee0 !important;
}
.item-chosen {
  background-color: #099 !important;
}
```

```
</style>

<script type="text/javascript">
  var highlightItem = 0;
  var chosenItem;

  window.addEventListener('load', function() {
    document.addEventListener('keydown', function(e) {
      var dir;
      if (e.keyCode == 38) {
        // Left arrow key
        dir = -1;
      } else if (e.keyCode == 40) {
        // Right arrow key
        dir = 1;
      } else if (e.keyCode == 13) {
        // User pressed ENTER
        var content = document.getElementById('content');
        var items =
            document.querySelectorAll('div.scroll-container > div');
        content.innerHTML = "You chose item "
            + items[highlightItem].innerHTML;
        if (chosenItem != undefined) {
          items[chosenItem].className =
              items[chosenItem].className.replace(/\s*item-chosen\s*/g, '');
        }
        chosenItem = highlightItem;
        items[chosenItem].className += ' item-chosen';
      }

      if (dir) {
        moveSelection(dir);
      }
    });
    moveSelection(0);
  });

  function moveSelection(dir) {
    // Get an array of all items in the list.
    var items =
        document.querySelectorAll('div.scroll-container > div');
    if (highlightItem + dir < 0 || highlightItem + dir >= items.length) {
      // Prevent movement from going off either end of the list of items.
      return;
    }
    // Unhighlight the currently highlighted item.
    items[highlightItem].className =
        items[highlightItem].className.replace(/\s*item-highlight\s*/, '');

    // Move to the next item in the requested direction.
    highlightItem += dir;

    // Highlight the new item.
    var item = items[highlightItem];
    item.className += ' item-highlight';
```

```
      }
    </script>
  </head>

  <body>
    <div class="scroll-container">
      <div>One</div>
      <div>Two</div>
      <div>Three</div>
      <div>Four</div>
      <div>Five</div>
    </div>
    <div>
      <p id="content">Highlight an item and press ENTER to choose.</p>
    </div>
  </body>
</html>
```

Paging Content

Horizontal Scrolling

Horizontal scrolling lists of items are a fairly common approach to providing large lists
of items in a format that can be easily navigated using the D-pad (Figure 5-7). The user
moves the left/right arrow keys to change the highlight in the list, and the list scrolls to
make sure that the highlighted item is visible. Generally, the scrolling is done with a
transition to provide a visual cue to what movement is happening.

Figure 5-7. A horizontal scrolling list

At the ends of the list, the designer may wish to wrap to the other end (again, transitions
provide a visual cue to what is going on). Items in the list might scroll off the page at
the right end, or the last item in the list might be anchored to the right side of the page.

There are a number of approaches to maintaining the highlight. The highlight can move
freely in the list, only causing it to scroll when the sides of the page are reached, or it
might stay in one place (e.g., the visual middle of the page) and the list might scroll
underneath it.

The code that follows demonstrates a straightforward implementation of a horizonal
scrolling list. Left and right arrow keys move the highlight through the items. The
highlighted item is always the leftmost item on the page.

The horizontal list is set up using a few important CSS property settings:

- Each item is displayed in an element using `display: inline-block`, which preserves the block properties of the DIV while providing inline arrangement.
- The item container uses `-webkit-transition: 1s left ease-in-out` to make sure that container movement smoothly animates when the CSS left property is changed.

  The inline-block setting on the contained elements would normally cause the container to insert a visual placeholder between each element. Since this placeholder is not a measurable value of each element, it's difficult to compute scroll distance. Setting `font-size: 0px;` eliminates this placeholder spacing.

  Finally, it sets `white-space: nowrap` to prevent the elements in the container (which are being laid out as inline elements because of inline-block) from wrapping at the window boundary as they normally would.
- The overall container uses `overflow: hidden` to make sure that elements that won't fit in the window will be clipped at its boundaries. Without this, the browser would create a scrollbar for the window.

```html
<html>
  <head>
    <style type="text/css">
      div.scroll-container > div > div {
        display: inline-block;
        background-color: #333;
        color: #eee;
        width: 100px;
        height: 100px;
        padding: 5px;
        font-size: 16px;
        border: 5px solid #eee;
      }
      div.scroll-container > div {
        position: relative;
        -webkit-transition: 1s left ease-in-out;
        font-size: 0px;
        white-space: nowrap;
      }
      div.scroll-container {
        overflow: hidden;
      }
      .item-highlight {
        border-color: #0e0 !important;
      }
    </style>

    <script type="text/javascript">
      var highlightItem = 0;

      window.addEventListener('load', function() {
        enableScrolling();
      });
```

```
    function enableScrolling() {
      document.addEventListener('keydown', function(e) {
        var dir;
        if (e.keyCode == 37) {
          // Left arrow key
          dir = -1;
        } else if (e.keyCode == 39) {
          // Right arrow key
          dir = 1;
        }

        if (dir) {
          moveSelection(dir);
        }
      });
      // Initialize selection at leftmost item.
      moveSelection(0);
    }

    function moveSelection(dir) {
      // Get an array of all items in the list.
      var items =
          document.querySelectorAll('div.scroll-container > div > div');
      if (highlightItem + dir < 0 || highlightItem + dir >= items.length) {
        // Prevent movement from going off either end of the list of items.
        return;
      }
      // Unhighlight the currently highlighted item.
      items[highlightItem].className =
          items[highlightItem].className.replace(/\s*item-highlight\s*/, '');

      // Move to the next item in the requested direction.
      highlightItem += dir;

      // Highlight the new item.
      var item = items[highlightItem];
      item.className += ' item-highlight';

      // Move the container of items far enough in the correct direction
      // to make the new item visible.
      var itemWidth = item.offsetWidth;
      var container = document.querySelector('div.scroll-container > div');
      var left = parseInt(container.style.left) || 0;
      container.style.left = left - (itemWidth * dir) + 'px';
    }
  </script>
</head>

<body>
  <div class="scroll-container">
    <div>
      <div>1</div>
      <div>2</div>
      <div>3</div>
      <div>4</div>
```

```
        <div>5</div>
        <div>6</div>
        <div>7</div>
        <div>8</div>
        <div>9</div>
        <div>10</div>
        <div>11</div>
        <div>12</div>
        <div>13</div>
        <div>14</div>
        <div>15</div>
      </div>
    </div>
  </body>
</html>
```

Vertical Scrolling

Vertical scrolling lists of items (Figure 5-8) meet a similar need to horizontal lists, but can also be used as a way to control the scrolling of content that extends beyond the bottom of a page. Using this approach, a page can provide large lists of items in a format that can be easily navigated using the D-pad. The user moves the up/down arrow keys to change the highlight in the list, and the list scrolls to make sure that the highlighted item is visible. Generally, the scrolling is done with a transition to provide a visual cue to what movement is happening.

At the top or bottom ends of the list, you may wish to wrap to the other end (again, transitions provide a visual cue to what is going on). Items in the list might scroll off the page at the bottom end, or the last item in the list might be anchored to the bottom of the page.

There are a number of approaches to maintaining the highlight. The highlight can move freely in the list, only causing it to scroll when the sides of the page are reached, or it might stay in one place (e.g., the visual middle of the page) and the list might scroll underneath it.

The code that follows demonstrates a straightforward implementation of a vertical scrolling list. Up and down arrow keys move the highlight (i.e., focus) through the items. The highlighted item is always the topmost item on the page.

The vertical list is set up using a few important CSS property settings:

- The item container uses `-webkit-transition: 1s top ease-in-out` to make sure that container movement smoothly animates when the CSS top property is changed.
- The overall container has its height set as `height: 100%` so that it fills the window vertically but does not extend beyond the window's lower boundary and trigger the creation of a scrollbar.

Highlight an item and press ENTER to choose.

Figure 5-8. A vertical scrolling list

Setting float: left; allows other elements on the page to flow to the right of the scrolling list.

- The HTML and body elements are given height: 100% so that the height set in the overall container is used by the browser. (Percentage heights are only used for an element if the parent element also sets a height.)

```
<html>
  <head>
    <style type="text/css">
      html, body {
        height: 100%;
        overflow: hidden;
      }
      div.scroll-container > div > div {
```

```css
    background-color: #333;
    color: #eee;
    width: 100px;
    height: 100px;
    padding: 5px;
    font-size: 20px;
    border: 5px solid #eee;
  }
  div.scroll-container > div {
    position: relative;
    -webkit-transition: 1s top ease-in-out;
  }
  div.scroll-container {
    height: 100%;
    float: left;
  }
  .item-highlight {
    border-color: #0e0 !important;
  }
</style>

<script type="text/javascript">
  var highlightItem = 0;

  window.addEventListener('load', function() {
    enableScrolling();
  });

  function enableScrolling() {
    document.addEventListener('keydown', function(e) {
      var dir;
      if (e.keyCode == 38) {
        // Left arrow key
        dir = -1;
      } else if (e.keyCode == 40) {
        // Right arrow key
        dir = 1;
      } else if (e.keyCode == 13) {
        // User pressed ENTER
        var content = document.getElementById('content');
        var items =
            document.querySelectorAll('div.scroll-container > div > div');
        content.innerHTML = "You chose item "
            + items[highlightItem].innerHTML;
      }

      if (dir) {
        moveSelection(dir);
      }
    });
    moveSelection(0);
  }

  function moveSelection(dir) {
    // Get an array of all items in the list.
```

```
        var items =
            document.querySelectorAll('div.scroll-container > div > div');
        if (highlightItem + dir < 0 || highlightItem + dir >= items.length) {
          // Prevent movement from going off either end of the list of items.
          return;
        }
        // Unhighlight the currently highlighted item.
        items[highlightItem].className =
            items[highlightItem].className.replace(/\s*item-highlight\s*/, '');

        // Move to the next item in the requested direction.
        highlightItem += dir;

        // Highlight the new item.
        var item = items[highlightItem];
        item.className += ' item-highlight';

        // Move the container of items far enough in the correct direction
        // to make the new item visible.
        var itemHeight = item.offsetHeight;
        var container = document.querySelector("div.scroll-container > div");
        var top = parseInt(container.style.top) || 0;
        container.style.top = top - (itemHeight * dir) + 'px';
      }
    </script>
  </head>

  <body>
    <div class="scroll-container">
      <div>
        <div>1</div>
        <div>2</div>
        <div>3</div>
        <div>4</div>
        <div>5</div>
        <div>6</div>
        <div>7</div>
        <div>8</div>
        <div>9</div>
        <div>10</div>
        <div>11</div>
        <div>12</div>
        <div>13</div>
        <div>14</div>
        <div>15</div>
      </div>
    </div>
    <div>
      <p id="content">Highlight an item and press ENTER to choose.</p>
    </div>
  </body>
</html>
```

Multiple Pages

Collections of larger items in a window, such as thumbnails, are often better shown in grids with multiple rows and columns, broken up into distinct pages of content. Users navigate between the thumbnails using the D-pad arrow keys. If they move "off" the left or right side of the page, content on the previous or next page is scrolled into view.

The code that follows demonstrates a potential implementation of a multiple page control design (Figure 5-9). It chooses to have the logical pages, each with a pre-defined number of rows and columns, laid out inline next to each other as if each page were an item in a horizontal scrolling row.

Figure 5-9. A multipage scrolling list

A new complication of the multipage design is the need to navigate with the D-pad horizontally and vertically, between items that are next to each other visually but not next to each other in the DOM structure, and between items that have different parents (that is, between items on different pages).

The approach the code takes for key navigation is to use Euclidean distance calculations to find the nearest item element in the direction of navigation, and then, if it finds that the item is on a different page, shift to that page. The distance calculation used is simplified for example purposes, and it only calculates distance from the top left corner of each element. In a more complex layout, where the controls are not in a regular grid, this method will not produce reliable results.

The multipage display is set up using a few important CSS property settings:

- The border for the selected item in this page is done by having slightly smaller DIV (with the actual contents in it) centered over a parent DIV. When the background color of the parent DIV changes, it appears to be a border around the child. This was done so that all sizes could be provided in percentages.

- The individual pages contain DIVs set with `float: left` so that they flow into the page. The width and height of these DIVs, given in percentages, determines the number of rows and columns per page. Currently, the setting of `width: 50%` and `height: 50%` provides two rows and two columns.

- As mentioned earlier, the pages are arranged using `display: inline-block` as if they were individual items in a row.

```
<html>
  <head>
    <style type="text/css">
      div.scroll-container > div > div > div > div {
        background-color: #333;
        color: #eee;
        width: 96%;
        height: 96%;
        top: 2%;
        left: 2%;
        position: relative;
      }
      div.scroll-container > div > div > div {
        float: left;
        background-color: #aaa;
        width: 50%;
        height: 50%;
      }
      div.scroll-container > div > div {
        display: inline-block;
        white-space: normal;
        font-size: 24px;
        width: 100%;
        height: 100%;
      }
      div.scroll-container > div {
        position: relative;
        -webkit-transition: 1s left ease-in-out;
        white-space: nowrap;
        width: 100%;
        height: 100%;
        font-size: 0px;
      }
      div.scroll-container {
        -webkit-box-shadow: 0px 0px 5px 6px #777;
        position: absolute;
        overflow: hidden;
        width: 50%;
        height: 50%;
```

```
      }
  .item-highlight {
    background-color: #0e0 !important;
  }
</style>

<script type="text/javascript">
  var highlightItem = 0;

  window.addEventListener('load', function() {
    enableScrolling();
  });

  function enableScrolling() {
    document.addEventListener('keydown', function(e) {
      var dirX = 0;
      var dirY = 0;
      if (e.keyCode == 37) {
        // Left arrow key
        dirX = -1;
      } else if (e.keyCode == 39) {
        // Right arrow key
        dirX = 1;
      } else if (e.keyCode == 38) {
        // Up arrow key
        dirY = -1;
      } else if (e.keyCode == 40) {
        // Down arrow key
        dirY = 1;
      }

      if (dirX || dirY) {
        moveSelection(dirX, dirY);
      }
    });
    moveSelection(0, 0);
  }

  function sign(val) {
    if (val > 0) {
      return 1;
    } else if (val < 0) {
      return -1;
    }
    return 0;
  }

  function calcDistance(from, to, dirX, dirY) {
    var fromLeft = from.offsetLeft + from.parentElement.offsetLeft;
    var fromTop = from.offsetTop + from.parentElement.offsetTop;

    var toLeft = to.offsetLeft + to.parentElement.offsetLeft;
    var toTop = to.offsetTop + to.parentElement.offsetTop;

    var dx = toLeft - fromLeft;
```

```
        var dy = toTop - fromTop;

        if (sign(dx) != dirX || sign(dy) != dirY)
          return -1;

        var distance = Math.sqrt((dx * dx) + (dy * dy));
        return distance;
      }

    function moveSelection(dirX, dirY) {
      // Get an array of all items in the list.
      var items =
          document.querySelectorAll("div.scroll-container > div > div > div");

      // Unhighlight the currently highlighted item.
      var currentItem = items[highlightItem];
      currentItem.className =
          currentItem.className.replace(/\s*item-highlight\s*/, '');

      // Loop through all items, looking for the closest item in the
      // correct direction of movement.
      var minDist;
      var newHighlightItem = highlightItem;
      for (var i = 0; i < items.length; i++) {
        var dist = calcDistance(currentItem, items[i], dirX, dirY);
        if (dist > 0 && (minDist == undefined || dist < minDist)) {
          minDist = dist;
          newHighlightItem = i;
        }
      }

      highlightItem = newHighlightItem;

      // Get an array of all the pages. Use the number of items on the
      // first page to calculate the page number the highlighted item is on.
      var pageContainers =
          document.querySelectorAll("div.scroll-container > div > div");
      var pageNum = Math.floor(highlightItem /
          pageContainers[0].children.length);

      // Highlight the new item.
      var item = items[highlightItem];
      item.className += ' item-highlight';

      // Move the container of items far enough in the correct direction
      // to make the new item visible.
      var container = document.querySelector("div.scroll-container > div");
      var pageLeft = pageContainers[pageNum].offsetLeft;
      var left = parseInt(container.style.left) || 0;
      container.style.left = -pageLeft + 'px';
    }
  </script>
</head>

<body>
```

```
<div class="scroll-container">
  <div>
  <div class="page-container">
    <div><div>1</div></div>
    <div><div>2</div></div>
    <div><div>3</div></div>
    <div><div>4</div></div>
  </div>
  <div class="page-container">
    <div><div>5</div></div>
    <div><div>6</div></div>
    <div><div>7</div></div>
    <div><div>8</div></div>
  </div>
  <div class="page-container">
    <div><div>9</div></div>
    <div><div>10</div></div>
    <div><div>11</div></div>
    <div><div>12</div></div>
  </div>
  <div class="page-container">
    <div><div>13</div></div>
    <div><div>14</div></div>
    <div><div>15</div></div>
  </div>
  </div>
  </div>
</body>
</html>
```

Using the knowledge you've gained in the previous two chapters and this chapter you now have a good sense for the different pieces that will be needed to build that killer web app. As you may have noticed, building web apps for Google TV does not rely on new technologies or rare techniques, but rather it is based on nuances and modifications to the way that web apps for the 2-foot experience are developed.

However, we're not done yet. In the next chapter, we'll be shifting our focus from the web app to content, and we'll discuss how to tune and optimize your videos, an important factor for web apps that present this type of content.

CHAPTER 6

Tuning, Delivering, and Protecting Video Content

Now that you've learned how to design and develop for the 10-foot UI experience, we'll turn to the most popular content consumed on TV: video. Whenever it comes to video content, developers and publishers on the web have many factors to take into consideration in order to ensure a good experience for users. This is especially important on Google TV because the video experience on big display devices like Google TV is expected to emulate, if not rival, the generally accepted viewing experience of high definition TV (HDTV).

To really achieve the best video experience possible, you'll need to develop a good understanding of video delivery and make intelligent trade-offs among many variables. For example, you'll need to learn about digitizing and editing your videos, choosing encoding formats, evaluating license and support issues, and selecting delivery options and protocols. You'll also need to learn about how to optimize video based on factors such as compression quality, frames per second, pixel resolution, bit rate, and bandwidth.

Before we discuss these key factors and how they play out on Google TV, however, we'll briefly recap some video basics.

Video Basics

Raw video files are ideal as far as video quality is concerned, but their sheer size usually hinders the speed and performance needed for online video, and also results in high storage and bandwidth costs. Subsequently, all web videos files are served in compressed or encoded formats. The process of video encoding is illustrated in Figure 6-1.

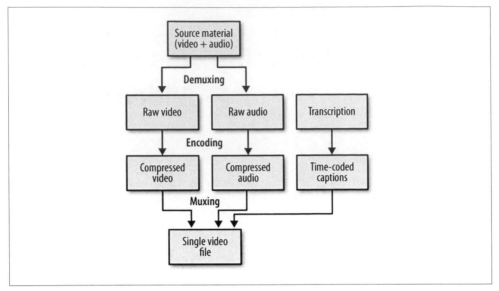

Figure 6-1. Video processing involves several steps, including demuxing and muxing

There are three main steps for turning source material of video and audio into a single video file:

1. *Demuxing*: separates out video and audio streams
2. *Encoding*: compresses video and audio streams
3. *Muxing*: combines video and audio streams plus captions (if any)

Note that text transcription can optionally be converted into time-coded captions and added into the mix to yield a single final video file during the step of muxing. There are four main concepts in video encoding:

1. *Video codec format*: defines how pixels are compressed
2. *Audio codec format*: defines how waveforms are compressed
3. *Caption format*: defines if and when captions are displayed
4. *Video container format*: holds it all together (think about zip format)

The video container formats define how video and audio are packaged together and they are commonly shown as the suffix of video files, therefore often referred to as video formats. Popular container formats include AVI, MP4, OGG, and FLV. Each has its own compatible audio and video codecs and caption formats, as detailed in the comparison found at *http://goo.gl/G0q01.*[*]

---

[*] Note that some codecs may be protected by patents or other intellectual property rights; you should get appropriate legal advice and information to help you determine if you need to seek a license for any particular codec.

On Google TV, there are two options for serving video content with a web app:

1. Embed video using HTML5 in a web page in Google Chrome
2. Embed video using the Flash Player plug-in in Google Chrome

Next, let's go over each one of these options and discuss specific recommendations in terms of encoding codecs and container formats, as well as optimization and tuning techniques.

Embedding Video with HTML5 in Google Chrome

Prior to the advent of HTML5, there was no standards-based way to achieve video content delivery. Instead, video "on the web" typically was funneled through a third party plug-in, such as QuickTime or Flash Player.

HTML5 introduced the <video> element, which allows developers to include video directly in web pages without using any plug-ins. Moreover, since the <video> tag is a part of the HTML5 specification, it enables deep and natural integration with the other layers of the web development stack, such as CSS, Javascript, and other HTML tags (e.g., canvas). This potentially opens up opportunities for rich interactive applications that don't rely on any plug-ins.

The Markup

In the Google Chrome browser and other modern browsers, you can embed the HTML5 <video> tag as follows:

```
<video>
  <source src="movie.mp4" type='video/mp4; codecs="avc1.42E01E, mp4a.40.2"' />
  <source src="movie.webm" type='video/webm; codecs="vp8, vorbis"' />
</video>
```

Alternatively, you may use a single video format which makes the syntax very similar to the tag used below:

```
<video src="movie.webm"></video>
```

There are various ways that you can integrate <video> tag via HTML5, and we recommend that you check out the examples provided at HTML5rocks.com to get a better feel for how video can be embedded this way.

Container Formats and Codecs

As you can see, multiple <source> tags can be used in general to include multiple container formats as fallback types for a variety of browsers. On Google TV, however, in order to minimize hardware requirements and software complexity, it is recommended that the container format MP4, combined with the H.264 video codec and the AAC audio codec, be used as this is the most widely adopted combination for encoding video content. Additionally, hardware acceleration of H.264 decoding is built into Google TV to ensure good performance on big screen devices.

Encoding, Tuning, and All That

Aside from choosing your container format and video and audio codecs, there are other variables and considerations you need to take into account when encoding and tuning your video. The following are specific recommendations applicable for Google TV that you should keep in mind when encoding and tuning your video:

Video codec	H.264
Audio codec	AAC
Resolution	720p or 1080p
Frame rate	24 to 30 frames per second (FPS)
Combined bit rate	Up to 2 Mbps
Pixel aspect ratio	1x1

While the HTML5 delivery option offers a quick and simple way of embedding video with a native tag inside Google Chrome, there are some missing features such as access to microphone and camera, support for streaming, and content protection and rights management. If any of these features are critical to your application, you'll want to consider Flash as an alternative.

Embedding Video Using the Flash Player Plug-in in Google Chrome

Flash is another option that you can use to encode video content. Video content will be embedded inside a SWF video player, and rendered via the SWF file using the Flash Player plug-in, which is bundled with Google Chrome by default. Here are the typical steps you'll have to perform:

1. Encode raw video files into appropriate video formats (e.g. FLV and F4V)
2. Write video player in ActionScript and load encoded video files as video assets into the video player and generate a SWF file
3. Embed the SWF file inside a web page and render it using the Flash Player plug-in in Google Chrome

The Markup

The following code snippet shows a typical way of embedding a SWF file inside a web page:

```
<object classid="clsid:D27CDB6E-AE6D-11cf-96B8-444553540000"
codebase="http://download.macromedia.com/.../swflash.cab#version=6,0,29,0"
width="400"
height="400" >

<param name="movie" value="videoplayer.swf">
<param name="quality" value="high" >
<param name="LOOP" value="false">

<embed src="videoplayer.swf"
width="400"
height="400"
loop="false"
quality="high"
pluginspage="http://www.macromedia.com/go/getflashplayer"
type="application/x-shockwave-flash">
</ embed >

</ object >
```

The <object> tag in this code is for general compatibility with the Internet Explorer browser, but on Google TV, since Chrome is the only available browser, the <embed> tag alone is sufficient.

Container Formats and Codecs

The supported container formats for Flash Player include MP4, FLV, F4V, AVI, and ASF. For Google TV, we recommend the following combinations of container formats, video codec, audio codec, and caption format:

Container format	Video codec	Audio codec	Caption
MP4	H.264	AAC	MPEG-4 Timed Text
FLV	H.264	AAC	DXFP
F4V	H.264	AAC	(N/A)

Encoding and Tuning Guidelines

The following are guidelines for Google TV that you may keep in mind when encoding and tuning your video for Flash:

Video codec	H.264, Main or High Profile, progressive encoding
Audio codec	AAC-LC or AC3, 44.1kHz, Stereo
Resolution	720p or 1080p
Frame rate	24 to 30 frames per second (FPS)
Combined bit rate	Up to 2 Mbps (or higher depending on available bandwith)
Pixel aspect ratio	1×1

Video Player and Rendering Optimization

The standard way of playing back Flash video (i.e., FLV video files) in a video player via ActionScript is to instantiate a Video object:

```
/ AS3
var myVideo:Video = new Video();
addChild(myVideo);
var nc:NetConnection = new NetConnection();
nc.connect(null);
var ns:NetStream = new NetStream(nc);
myVideo.attachNetStream(ns);
ns.play("http://yourserver.com/flash-files/MyVideo.flv");
```

However, this generic Video object comes with many features, like rotation, blend-Mode, alpha channel, filter, mask, etc., that may be overkill for a high resolution display (they also tend to result in less than ideal performance, especially on a device using a less-powerful CPU). Because of this, Adobe introduced a new *StageVideo* API to improve video rendering on high-resolution devices like Google TV.

You can implement the StageVideo object using the following code:

```
var v:Vector.<StageVideo> = stage.stageVideos;
var stageVideo:StageVideo;
if ( v.length >= 1 ) {
    stageVideo=v[0];
}

netConnection = newNetConnection();
netConnection.connect(null);
netStream = new NetStream(netConnection);

var v:Vector.<StageVideo> = stage.stageVideos;
if ( v.length >= 1 ) {
    varstageVideo:StageVideo=v[0];
    stageVideo.viewPort=new Rectangle(100,100,320,240);
    stageVideo.addEventListener(StageVideoEvent.RENDER_STATE,<callback>);
    stageVideo.attachNetStream(netStream);
}
netStream.play("MyVideo.f4v")
```

By introducing StageVideo object, Adobe has made a trade-off in favor of performance at the expense of certain features. For example, on Google TV, the StageVideo object does not have alpha property for transparency and you cannot play multiple StageVideo objects simultaneously. You can read more about the StageVideo object on Adobe's website at *http://goo.gl/qXWoV*.

Video Delivery Guidelines

The Adobe Flash Platform offers a variety of protocols to support various applications that serve video over a network. These protocols include:

- HTTP Dynamic Streaming (F4F format)
- RTMP/e Streaming
- HTTP Progressive Download
- RTMFP Peer-to-Peer
- RTMFP Multicast

Depending on the nature of your applications and existing delivery infrastructure, you may want to choose your protocols appropriately. For example, you may want streaming video for real-time application or progressive download for faster playback or broadcast versus peer-to-peer video experiences. These options offer you a lot of flexibility and make it possible to develop applications that go beyond simple video playback.

Another aspect of your video delivery system over the Internet is that available bandwidth changes in real time throughout the time a video is playing back. For this reason, your delivery system needs to be smart enough to dynamically adjust bitrate.

On the server side, you could consider Adobe Flash Media Server technology, which offers adaptive bitrate capabilities as well as recovery during network outages.

Video Player and Rendering Optimizations

It is important to optimize your video player. If your video player hogs too many CPU cycles, it may affect the frame rate of the video playback, or it may cause the UI to feel sluggish and unresponsive. Typically, excessive script execution and excessive rendering are often culprits for poor user experiences.

Here are some considerations to keep in mind when developing your video player:

- Simplify rendering complexity: reduce the number of objects on Stage as much as possible
- Limit use of timer functions and check for duplicates; minimize ActionScript processing intervals
- Avoid render items not currently visible
- Cose the NetStream when video is finished
- Do not set wmode to "transparent" and avoid transparency in general
- Avoid executing large amount of script while video is playing back

Content Protection and DRM

Google TV supports Flash Platform content protection for premium video content. Many of the leading premium video providers use the Flash Platform to provide a seamless viewing experience.

Streaming video securely from Flash Media Server (FMS) is possible by using technologies such as RTMPE (Real Time Media Protocol Encrypted) and SWF Verification. The content protection features in FMS are supported by the vast majority of content delivery networks (CDNs), enabling an easy content workflow and broad geographical reach. See Adobe's white paper entitled *Protecting Online Video Distribution with Adobe Flash Media Technology*, for an overview of typical content protection workflows using RTMPE, SWF Verification, and related features: *http://goo.gl/93zHm*.

We also expect other available content protection mechanisms will be supported in future versions of Google TV.

 Remember to only present video and other content on your site that you have the legal right to use, and to get legal advice if you have any doubts about your ability to use specific content.

CHAPTER 7

Getting Your Content to the User: Discovery, Indexing, and Search Results

Help Users Discover Your Content

Armed with a quick search box (Figure 7-1) and the Google Chrome browser, users with Google TV are one query away from visiting your site. As you crafted your site for the 10-foot experience, it's smart to consider making a site that's search friendly so you can capitalize on traffic from the 40%+ increase[*] in Internet searches in recent years.

As we've already touched on in previous chapters, Google TV users view search results (Figure 7-2) that are a blend of:

- TV listings
- Videos indexed by Google Video Search
- Web search results (web pages, books, images, etc.)

This chapter focuses on helping you optimize your site for search, which ultimately will help users to find your web app and its content. We'll start by reviewing some basic information about how search engines work, then we'll cover some of the strategies and practices you can use for your own web app.

---

[*] http://www.comscore.com/Press_Events/Press_Releases/2010/1/Global_Search_Market_Grows_46_Percent_in_2009

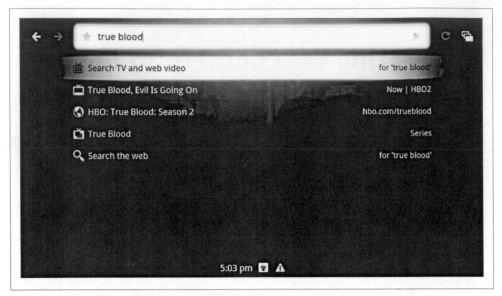

Figure 7-1. The Quick Search Box (QSB) on Google TV combines results from TV programs, videos, and web pages

Figure 7-2. In addition to performing regular web searches, Google TV users can also view TV and video specific search results; shown here are the results for videos for Google TV at the Google I/O conference

How Search Engines Work

Crawling, Indexing, Search Results

In a general sense, search engines have three main processes:

1. Crawling (retrieving a web page)
2. Indexing (making sense of the content of the page)
3. Search results (ordering and displaying results in a relevant manner for the user)

To make a site optimized for TV-based searches, you should employ best practices at every stage of the *search engine pipeline*. These practices are similar to those used for desktop sites, but it's worth reiterating them so that your TV web app is as search friendly as possible. We won't delve into the technical intricacies of search engine optimization (SEO), but you can learn more about this topic with Google's SEO resources for beginners listed at:

http://goo.gl/D8NFd

Please remember that the information we're providing is specific to Google Search, although many of our recommendations also apply to other popular search engines.

 The Googlebot is the name of Google's crawler. It's an automated process that fetches web content in compliance with the robots.txt specification. Please see "Controlling Crawling and Indexing," hosted on *http://code.google.com*, for information on preventing your content from being crawled.

http://goo.gl/hg7u4

Components of an Individual Search Result

Search results, whether for videos or web pages, have similar components (e.g., title and description). For reference, here's some of the terminology we'll use throughout the chapter.

Figure 7-3. Several components of a web search result

Site Architecture

Site architecture is the construction of your site, such as the directory structure and/or the internal linking schema.

Design a Logical Linking Structure

Here are some important considerations to keep in mind when designing an architecture helpful to both users and search engines:

- Check that users are able to easily navigate from the home page to individual pages and back again
- Verify that URLs are "shareable." Important pages can be linked to and referenced from one TV user to another.
- Avoid hiding your content from crawlers, such as making pages only accessible via a search box. Instead, internally link to content you want crawled and indexed by search engines.
- Prevent restrictions on crawlers, such as requiring a login or cookie to view public content. Crawlers more easily find content through public links not blocked by forms or cookies.

To verify whether the crawler (Googlebot, in this case) detected your links, check out the Webmaster Tools "Internal links" feature for your verified site (Figure 7-4).

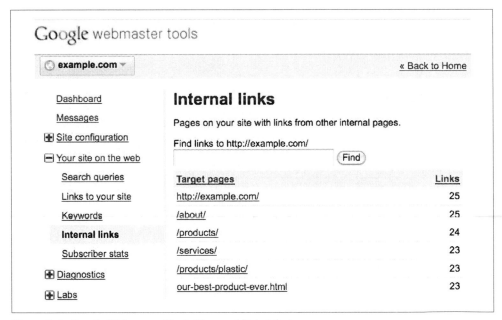

Figure 7-4. Google Webmaster Tools "Internal links" feature

You can learn more about internal links on Webmaster Tools at: *http://goo.gl/oyi7S*

 If you're using Ajax-based navigation, be sure to include capability for your users to share URLs and use back/forward buttons. Google supports the Ajax Crawling Scheme to help your Ajax site to be better crawled and indexed: *http://goo.gl/ceFQT*

Use Descriptive Anchor Text

Anchor text, the clickable words in a link, is a signal to search engines and users about the content of the target URL. The more search engines understand about your pages, such as the content, title, and in-bound anchor text, the more relevant information can be returned to searchers. Descriptive anchor text avoids phrases like "click here":

```
To view more cute kitten videos <a href="cute-kitten-videos.html">click here</a>.
```

And instead contains relevant keywords such as "cute kitten videos":

```
Feel free to browse our <a href="cute-kitten-videos.html">cute kitten videos</a>.
```

URL Structure

URL structure is important because in Google search results, the URL of a document is displayed to the user below the document's title and snippet. URLs that contain relevant keywords provide searchers with more information about the result—often in resulting in higher click-through. Additionally, for search engines, keywords in the URL can be used as a signal in ranking.

Include Keywords in the URL, If Possible

It's helpful for users to see their query terms reinforced in the search result. If the user queries [google webmaster blog], it's obvious the keywords "google," "webmaster," and, "blog" help signal to the user that the result is relevant.

Here are helpful URLs:

- *http://www.example.com/google-webmaster-blog*
- *http://www.example.com/page.php?company=google&type=webmaster&format=blog*

Not as helpful:

- *http://www.example.com/239rsk-00433.html.html*

Note that keywords in the URL that match the user's query are highlighted in the search result (Figure 7-5). Keywords are more descriptive than cryptic numbers and letters, which can go unnoticed in results (Figure 7-6).

google webmaster blog
Search
About 7,490,000 results (0.09 seconds)
Advanced search
Official Google Webmaster Central Blog
The official weblog on Google crawling and indexing, and on webmaster tools, including the Sitemaps facility.
googlewebmastercentral.blogspot.com/ - Cached - Similar
Google's SEO Starter Guide
Specify your canonical
Make your websites run faster ...
Quality links to your site
Using site speed in web search ranking
Introducing Rich Snippets
Improved Flash indexing
Facebook Share and RDFa
More results from blogspot.com »

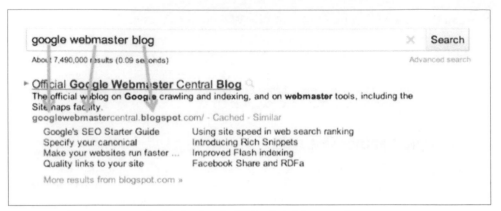

Figure 7-5. Query terms are highlighted in the URL—helpful to searchers

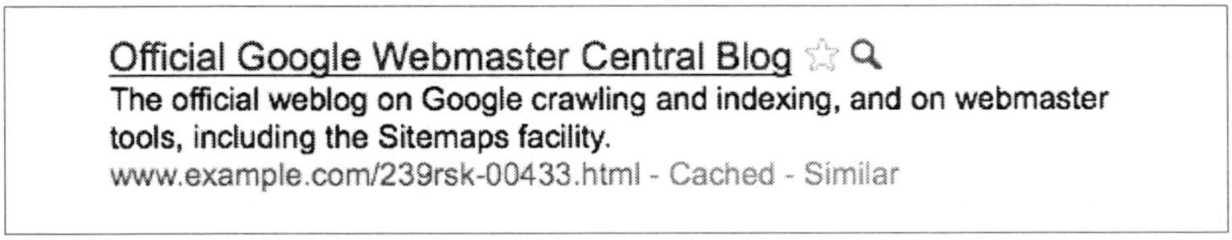

Official Google Webmaster Central Blog
The official weblog on Google crawling and indexing, and on webmaster tools, including the Sitemaps facility.
www.example.com/239rsk-00433.html - Cached - Similar

Figure 7-6. Cryptic filenames are less descriptive for searchers

Select the Right URL Structure for Your TV Site

When designing for TV, there are two general options for your URL structure:

1. Keep URL structure and site architecture the same in your TV and desktop versions. For example:

   Desktop and TV users both browse *http://www.example.com/article1*

2. Create new URLs for the TV version. This can be accomplished using relevant subfolders:

   Desktop users browse *http://www.example.com/article1*

   TV users browse *http://www.example.com/tv/article1*

   Or with subdomains:

   TV users browse *http://tv.example.com/article1*

Note that Google recommends the second option. Note that having multiple URLs for one piece of content (e.g., one URL for desktop users, one URL for TV users) will not cause duplicate content issues if `rel="canonical"` is implemented (see "Duplicate Content: Side Effects and Options" on page 90 for more on the canonical attribute).

Learn the Facts About Dynamic URLs

If your site uses dynamic URLs, Google provides a few pointers:

- Use name/value pairs such as item=car&type=sedan
- Be careful with URL rewriting—it's not uncommon for a developer to incorrectly implement URL rewrites, causing crawling and indexing issues for search engines
- Verify ownership of your site in Google Webmaster Tools and utilize the URL parameter handling feature to help Google crawl your site more efficiently (Figure 7-7).

Figure 7-7. For sites with dynamic URLs, Google Webmaster Tools' "parameter handling" allows the developer to specify to Googlebot which parameters to ignore when crawling

On-Page Optimizations

In addition to site architecture and URL structure, there are on-page optimizations which can improve your performance in search. For example, the first thing a user sees in search results is likely your page's title and a snippet. In many cases, you have some control over what is displayed. The key things to consider are:

- Are my page titles informative?
- Are my descriptions informative and compelling for the user?
- If I'm showing a video result, is the thumbnail and information about the video as accurate as possible?

Create Unique Titles Reflective of the Page's Content

`<titles>` are used as the first line of each search result. Using descriptive words and phrases in your page's title tag helps both users and search engines better understand the focus of the page (Figure 7-8 and Figure 7-9).

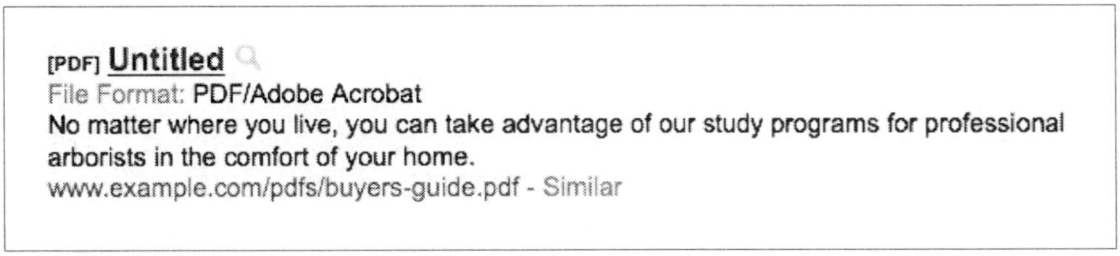

[PDF] **Untitled**
File Format: PDF/Adobe Acrobat
No matter where you live, you can take advantage of our study programs for professional arborists in the comfort of your home.
www.example.com/pdfs/buyers-guide.pdf - Similar

Figure 7-8. "Untitled" isn't a descriptive title

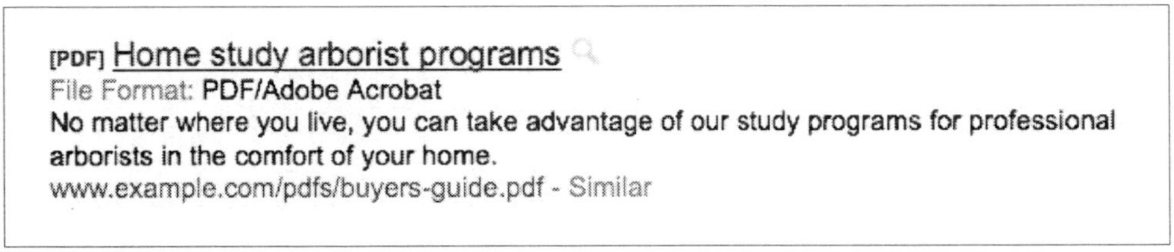

[PDF] Home study arborist programs
File Format: PDF/Adobe Acrobat
No matter where you live, you can take advantage of our study programs for professional arborists in the comfort of your home.
www.example.com/pdfs/buyers-guide.pdf - Similar

Figure 7-9. Descriptive titles help searchers

Include Unique Meta Descriptions for Each Page

Google often displays the description meta tag as the snippet of the search result. In other words, if it's relevant to the query, the meta description you create can be visible to the user. Similar to the <title> tag, the description meta tag is placed within the <head> tag of your HTML document. Whereas a page's title may be a few words or a phrase, a page's meta description may include several sentences.

Each page should have a unique description reflective of the content. Avoid "keyword stuffing" the description (e.g. <meta name="description" content="best video brad pitt tom cruise george clooney cute kitten three wolves shirt" />).

Google Webmaster Tools provides an "HTML Suggestions" section that provides information about titles and meta description that are either too short, long, or are duplicates (Figure 7-10).

Note that the <meta keywords> tag is not used as a signal to Google.

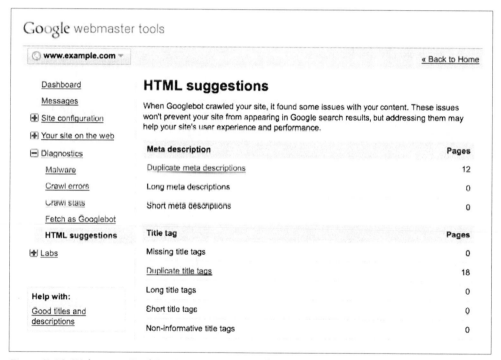

Figure 7-10. Webmaster Tools' "HTML suggestions" feature provides information on pages with suboptimal titles and meta descriptions

Duplicate Content: Side Effects and Options

It's likely that to properly serve users on different devices, you've created multiple URLs containing the same content. For example, these URLs may point to pages with the same (or extremely similar) main content but with a slightly different display or interaction:

- *http://www.example.com/tv/article1* for Google TV users
- *http://www.example.com/article1* for regular desktop users

In common search optimization (SEO) lingo, the same content available on different URLs is known as "duplicate content," an undesirable scenario. Although search engines already attempt to address duplicate content issues on their own, if you'd like to be more proactive, here are some steps to limit or reduce duplicate content:

1. Choose a version from the duplicate URLs as the canonical. This is likely the cleanest, most user-friendly version.
2. Be consistent with the canonical URL. Internal links should use this version, not any of the duplicates. Also, sitemaps submitted should only contain the canonical and exclude the duplicates.
3. On the duplicate URL, you may wish to include rel="canonical", listing the URL you'd prefer to appear in search results (i.e. the canonical).

   More information on duplicate content and `rel="canonical"` can be found at:

   http://goo.gl/kvfsz

 Google recommends that you do *not* robots.txt disallow the duplicate version of your content. If crawling is disallowed, Google cannot obtain a copy of the document, and the `rel="canonical"` hint will remain undetected.

Serving the Right Version to Your Users

Regardless if their device is a TV, desktop, or mobile phone, you want every visitor to your site to have the best possible experience. For instance, when a Google TV user clicks this URL in search results:

http://www.example.com/article1

(which is both the canonical version and the desktop version), instead of serving this desktop URL, serve the appropriate TV-based app at:

http://www.example.com/tv/article1

or

http://tv.example.com/article1

As discussed in Chapter 4, the *User-Agent string* can be used to detect whether your visitor comes from a Chrome browser on Google TV.

Working with Video: King of Content for TV

Much of this chapter has presented you with a number of ideas and approaches for producing and managing your content to maximize your site for search. Video content is one of the most popular rich media formats in the world, and every day, millions of people around the world access cool and engaging videos from a variety of sources. But with all of the content that's out there, how can you make sure that your videos are discovered by users? The first step in helping your viewers find that content is to have the content indexed.

Feeds

Crawling rich media content, such as videos, is difficult. You can complement this crawling process, ensuring that Google knows about all of your rich media content, by using a sitemap or media RSS (mRSS) feed. A Google Video Sitemap or mRSS feed enables you to provide descriptive information about your video content that can be indexed by Google's search engine. This metadata, such as a video's title, description, and duration, may be used in search results, thereby making it easier for users to find particular content.

 Media RSS, or mRSS, is an extension to RSS that is used to syndicate various types of multimedia, including audio, video, and images.

The Google Video Sitemap is an extension of the sitemap protocol. This protocol enables you to publish and syndicate online video content (and its relevant metadata) in order to make it searchable in a content-specific index known as the Google Video index. When Google's indexing servers become aware of a video sitemap, usually through submission via the Webmaster Tools, the sitemap is used to crawl your website and identify your videos.

A Google Video Sitemap is simply a link to each video landing page, along with some additional information, such as title, description, thumbnail, and duration, which can be displayed in the search results.

Before we dive into some key elements of the video feed, it's important to note that the video feed needs to be optimized for the search engine pipeline of crawling, indexing, and ranking. By including all of the video content on a site in a Google Video Sitemap, and subsequently submitting the video sitemap via the Webmaster Console, we can speed up the crawling process. As we add the necessary metadata for each of the videos, we're providing information for ranking, and writing content that will tell the user about the video in the results page.

Here is an example entry of a Google Video Sitemap for a page that included video:

```
<urlset xmlns="http://www.sitemaps.org/schemas/sitemap/0.9"
        xmlns:video="http://www.google.com/schemas/sitemap-video/1.1">
  <url>
    <loc>http://www.example.com/videos/some_video_landing_page.html</loc>
    <video:video>
      <video:thumbnail_loc>http://www.example.com/thumbs/123.jpg
      </video:thumbnail_loc>
      <video:title>Grilling steaks for summer</video:title>
      <video:description>Alkis shows you how to get perfectly done steaks every
        time</video:description>
      <video:content_loc>http://www.example.com/video123.flv</video:content_loc>
      <video:player_loc allow_embed="yes" autoplay="ap=1">
        http://www.example.com/videoplayer.swf?video=123</video:player_loc>
      <video:duration>600</video:duration>
      <video:expiration_date>2009-11-05T19:20:30+08:00</video:expiration_date>
      <video:rating>4.2</video:rating>
      <video:view_count>12345</video:view_count>
      <video:publication_date>2007-11-05T19:20:30+08:00</video:publication_date>
      <video:tag>steak</video:tag>
      <video:tag>meat</video:tag>
      <video:tag>summer</video:tag>
      <video:category>Grilling</video:category>
      <video:family_friendly>yes</video:family_friendly>
      <video:restriction relationship="allow">IE GB US CA</video:restriction>
      <video:gallery_loc title="Cooking Videos">http://cooking.example.com
      </video:gallery_loc>
      <video:price currency="EUR">1.99</video:price>
      <video:requires_subscription>yes</video:requires_subscription>
      <video:uploader info="http://www.example.com/users/userA">userA
        </video:uploader>
    </video:video>
  </url>
</urlset>
```

Required Tags

There are a number of key elements that should be included for each video:

Element	Description	Included in search results?
`<loc>`	The play page URL where users can watch the video	Included in the search results
`<video:thumbnail_loc>`	URL pointing to thumbnail image file to represent your video in search results. Most image sizes and types are accepted, but it is recommended that your thumbs be at least 160 × 120 pixels in .jpg, .png, or .gif formats.	May be included in the search results
`<video: title>`	Contains the title of the video and is limited to 100 characters.	May be included in the search results
`<video:description>`	Contains the description of the video and is limited to 2048 characters (longer descriptions will be truncated.)	May be included in the search results
`<video:content_loc>`	The URL should point to a .mpg, .mpeg, .mp4, .m4v, .mov, .wmv, .asf, .avi, .ra, .ram, .rm, .flv, or other video file format, and can be omitted if `<video:player_loc>` is specified. However, because Google needs to be able to check that the Flash object is actually a player for video (as opposed to some other use of Flash, e.g. games and animations), it's helpful to provide both.	NOT included in the search results
`<video:player_loc>`	A URL pointing to a Flash player for a specific video. In general, this is the information in the src element of an `<embed>` tag and should not be the same as the content of the `<loc>` tag. Since each video is uniquely identified by its content URL (the location of the actual video file) or, if a content URL is not present, a player URL (a URL pointing to a player for the video), you must include either the `<video:player_loc>` or `<video:content_loc>` tags. If these tags are omitted and we can't find this information, we'll be unable to index your video.	NOT included in the search results

The optional attribute `allow_embed` specifies whether Google can embed the video in search results. Allowed values are Yes or No.

The optional attribute `autoplay` has a user-defined string (in the previous example, ap = 1) that Google may append (if appropriate) to the flashvars parameter to enable autoplay of the video. For example: `<embed src="http://www.example.com/video player.swf?video=123" autoplay="ap=1"/>`.

Examples:

- YouTube: *http://www.youtube.com/v/v65Ud3VqChY*
- Dailymotion: *http://www.dailymotion.com/swf/x1o2g*

Help ensure that only Googlebot accesses your content by using a reverse DNS lookup (*http://www.google.com/support/webmasters/bin/answer.py?answer=80553*).

When you submit a Google Video Sitemap via the Webmaster Tools, you start the search engine pipeline. Each video item will be parsed, identified, and the corresponding content page will be fetched. After each page is fetched, a validation process takes place to ensure that the data in the Google Video Sitemap feed matches that on the play page and that the page contains a video. If validation is successful, the feed data may either be inserted into the index (if this is a new page) or an existing page may be updated.

 While the video sitemap may make it easier for the Googlebot to find content that it would not otherwise discover, it does not guarantee that all videos included in the sitemap will appear in the search results.

Optional Tags

In addition to optimizing the search engine pipeline process and the user experience on your site, you should pay attention to the user experience on a search engine results page. Remember that time when you did a search to find that long lost video about a dog surfing? Then when you got the search results back, you clicked on a link, only to find a "Sorry this video is not available" message.

As the content provider and submitter of the video feed, you can prevent some of that poor user experience by using some optional tags in Google Video Sitemaps.

`<video:expiration_date>`	If you have content that expires, you can submit this tag with the date after which the video will no longer be available, in W3C format. Acceptable values are complete date (YYYY-MM-DD) and complete date plus hours, minutes and seconds, and timezone (YYYY-MM-DDThh:mm:ss+TZD). For example, 2007-07-16T19:20:30+08:00.
	Is is recommended that you not supply this information if your video does not expire.
`<video:publica tion_date>`	A complementary tag that can be used which can help in the Google Video Sitemap management. For example, if publish your video sitemap periodically, and content will not be available until some time in between your sitemap updates, you can use this tag to tell Google to index the video, but not show it in search results until after this date.
	Acceptable values are complete date (YYYY-MM-DD) and complete date plus hours, minutes and seconds, and timezone (YYYY-MM-DDThh:mm:ss+TZD). For example, 2007-07-16T19:20:30+08:00.
`<video:duration>`	Contains the duration of the video in seconds. This will be presented in the search results, and can be used by the user to filter results by video length.
	Value must be between 0 and 28800 (8 hours). Only digit characters are allowed.

In addition to limiting access to content temporally, access may be restricted based on geographic location. For example, video content produced in the UK may only be viewable to users in the UK. Thus, you would not want someone in Japan to see the page in her search results. This can be managed using the `<video:restriction>` tag.

`<video:restriction>`	A list of countries where the video may or may not be played, in space-delimited ISO 3166 format. The required attribute "relationship" specifies whether the video is restricted or permitted for the specified countries. Allowed values are allow or deny. Only one `<video:restriction>` tag can appear for each video. If there is no `<video:restriction>` tag, it is assumed that the video can be played in all territories.

Other Feeds/Options

Video Sitemap or mRSS

If you're further wondering about the benefits of specific feeds (video sitemaps versus mRSS), we can provide some clarification. First, you should note that you can use either. Neither format gets priority or precedence over the other. However, one benefit of video sitemaps is that the format can quickly be extended to allow for more specifications, as Google maintains the format.

 If you're going to start from scratch, video sitemaps is the recommended approach.

Facebook Share and RDFs

You can expand the metadata about content on your pages with the use of markup tags in the body of the web page. Google recognizes two video markup formats: Facebook Share and Yahoo! SearchMonkey RDFa. Using either (or both) of these formats to mark up video directly in your HTML enables the Googlebot to better understand and present video content. Be sure that this additional markup appears in the HTML without the execution of JavaScript or Flash as otherwise the information will not be discoverable.

TV Show Tags

If your site contains episodic content (like television shows), you can provide Google additional information about those videos to further enhance the user's search experience. Figure 7-11 demonstrates this experience and the results for the first season of the TV show "House."

Figure 7-11. Screenshot example with episodic content

You can see that Google presents all of the House Season 1 episodes that have been indexed. In the navigation pane on the left, you can easily select other seasons and look at those results as well.

Adding the TV show metadata is accomplished by adding a `<video:tvshow>` tag along with the relevant children tags as demonstrated below:

```
<video:video>
  <video:title>My Super Show, Season 1, Episode 2</video:title>
  ... other required root level video tags ...
  <video:tvshow>
    <video:show_title>The Super Show</video:show_title>
    <video:video_type>full</video:video_type>
    <video:episode_title>The Best Show Ever</video:episode_title>
    <video:season_number>1</video:season_number>
    <video:episode_number>3</video:episode_number>
  </video:tvshow>
</video:video>
```

Full details for the TV show tags (for both Google Video Sitemaps and Bing mRSS feed) can be found at *http://goo.gl/Gi2nW*.

What's Next?

Now that you have a full, end-to-end understanding of the platform and the technical skills needed to build web apps for Google TV, it's time for you to put your knowledge into action. Think about the types of experiences that you want to deliver on the big screen and start building them.

We've touched on the fundamental techniques and skills needed to build web apps, but we're counting on you to innovate and deliver compelling experiences that truly transform TV. Once you've built your web app, spread the word about it and help users discover what you created. Aside from ensuring that your site is easily searched and indexed, be sure to let other developers know about your web app in the Google TV web forum (*http://goo.gl/pR9UB*) and submit your app to the Google TV web app gallery (*http://gtv-gallery.appspot.com/*).

Onward and upward!

About the Authors

Andrés is a Developer Advocate for Google's Developer Relations team. Prior to joining Google, Andrés founded Cartosoft, a geospatial solutions provider. Prior to his work on Cartosoft, Andres served as Vice President of Operations for Geographic Technologies Group, a leading provider of geospatial services and software for local governments throughout the United States. Andres has worked in the public, private, and nonprofit sectors, and his experience includes working for various startups, metropolitan planning organizations (MPOs), The World Bank, and as a volunteer for various nonprofits.

Amanda currently leads developer relations efforts for Google TV, YouTube, and Video Search. She's been at Google since 2006 and has had the privilege to work on various products, including Google Apps, App Engine, and Google Wave. Previously, she held various engineering roles at Bank of America and AT&T.

Daniels is a Developer Programs Engineer who's had the pleasure of working with several developer communities since he joined Google in 2006. After starting with iGoogle gadgets, he worked closely with advertisers and agencies via Gadget Ads, then onto Geo APIs focusing on V2 to V3 migration, and now Google TV.

Maile coordinates Webmaster Central outreach efforts as a Developer Advocate based in Mountain View, California. She manages the Webmaster Central Blog—teaching developers, SEOs, publishers, and hobbyists to create a search-friendly website. She'd argue with her colleagues that Search is "where it's at." Previously, Maile was a systems integration consultant for several pharmaceutical and technology companies, as well as for the Department of Defense.

As a Developer Advocate, Paul works to promote Google's APIs and technologies. He is currently engaging with partners to develop video sitemaps to improve Video Search. At Google, he has managed a number of internal technical support teams, Google Analytics Support and developed data warehousing solutions enabling Google's Sales and Support teams to scale.

Shawn is a Developer Advocate at Google. He works on Google TV and Google Maps APIs, but previously worked on OpenSocial APIs for social applications. Prior to joining Google in 2008, he worked at Yahoo, Ariba, eBay, and a few early startups.

Steve has been a software engineer for twenty-five years, starting his career with the brilliant but doomed Commodore Amiga. Prior to joining Google, Steve worked as a master software architect at Hewlett-Packard. His programming experience ranges from C/C++ to JavaScript.

Colophon

The animal on the cover of *Building Web Apps for Google TV*, first edition, is a musk deer.

The cover image is from *Cassell's Natural History*. The cover font is Adobe ITC Garamond. The text font is Linotype Birka; the heading font is Adobe Myriad Condensed; and the code font is LucasFont's TheSansMonoCondensed.

Get even more for your money.

Join the O'Reilly Community, and register the O'Reilly books you own. It's free, and you'll get:

- $4.99 ebook upgrade offer
- 40% upgrade offer on O'Reilly print books
- Membership discounts on books and events
- Free lifetime updates to ebooks and videos
- Multiple ebook formats, DRM FREE
- Participation in the O'Reilly community
- Newsletters
- Account management
- 100% Satisfaction Guarantee

Signing up is easy:

1. **Go to: oreilly.com/go/register**
2. **Create an O'Reilly login.**
3. **Provide your address.**
4. **Register your books.**

Note: English-language books only

To order books online:
oreilly.com/store

For questions about products or an order:
orders@oreilly.com

To sign up to get topic-specific email announcements and/or news about upcoming books, conferences, special offers, and new technologies:
elists@oreilly.com

For technical questions about book content:
booktech@oreilly.com

To submit new book proposals to our editors:
proposals@oreilly.com

O'Reilly books are available in multiple DRM-free ebook formats. For more information:
oreilly.com/ebooks

Spreading the knowledge of innovators   oreilly.com

The information you need, when and where you need it.

With Safari Books Online, you can:

Access the contents of thousands of technology and business books

- Quickly search over 7000 books and certification guides
- Download whole books or chapters in PDF format, at no extra cost, to print or read on the go
- Copy and paste code
- Save up to 35% on O'Reilly print books
- **New!** Access mobile-friendly books directly from cell phones and mobile devices

Stay up-to-date on emerging topics before the books are published

- Get on-demand access to evolving manuscripts.
- Interact directly with authors of upcoming books

Explore thousands of hours of video on technology and design topics

- Learn from expert video tutorials
- Watch and replay recorded conference sessions

Lightning Source UK Ltd.
Milton Keynes UK
UKOW011219260213

206835UK00004B/189/P